Teach Your Child English

Fun One to One English Teaching Games For Parents and Private Tutors of ESL

SHELLEY ANN VERNON

ACKNOWLEDGEMENTS

THANKS TO TWO OF MY PUPILS ANNA AND JULIE FOR STARRING IN THE ONLINE VIDEO DEMONSTRATION LESSONS THAT ARE INCLUDED WITH THIS BOOK.

CONTENTS

INTRODUCTION

It's a joy and a pleasure to spend time with a child. Children are so easy to please when they are the centre of attention and even the simplest game is fun for them. Young children have no problem putting themselves into an imaginary setting, so some spoons can become a sorcerer's treasure in the blink of an eye. Be light hearted and playful. Soon you will be rewarded with the immense satisfaction of seeing your child or pupil becoming a confident English speaker, knowing it was thanks to you.

The number one golden rule is always to encourage your pupil. Never let on if you think your pupil should be learning faster, or should know more. This will only make him or her feel inadequate and discouraged. You can even put a child off from learning English for life if you let slip any negativity in this way. This is a CLASSIC error when it comes to parents, who usually have unrealistic, even ridiculous expectations about "their little Einstein" who really should be fluent by day three. The child will think English is too difficult and say he or she does not like it as a defence. Learning and enjoyment are connected so it's up to you to create the right kind of safe environment through your attitude.

Another golden rule is to observe. Through careful observation you will see if the child is coping well, is becoming uncertain, whether you need to step up the pace or simplify.

The games in this book are meant for age three and up as the games are too structured for toddlers but you may be able to start using some of them from two and a half. All children are different and one of the big advantages of teaching one on one is that you may tailor things to exactly suit your pupil. If you are teaching a two year old child then there is a special report on teaching twos included with my first set of preschool stories, or available separately if you email me on info@teachingenglishgames.com for details.

The video session I did with Anna was longer than I would normally make a lesson because I wanted to get the story in. If I had not been filming I might not have done as many animals, probably only 5 rather than 7, because it was slightly too much for her. Despite that, after lunch while I was doing Julie's lesson, Anna spent the afternoon showing her mum all the games and playing them with her. She absolutely loved spending quality time with here mum and being the centre of attention. You too can have quality time with your child, playing together and imparting your knowledge of English at the same time. If you watch the video with Anna you'll see that all you need are a few pieces of paper with pictures, and the games are so easy to do! So really nothing should hold you back from getting started helping your child become bilingual today..

Using the Videos

The videos show lessons with Anna, just turned 6, and Julie, aged 12. These lessons are totally natural and unedited so you can see really and truly how the lessons went. The children did not know what we would be doing and were not prepared in any way for the session - other than to put on their fancy clothes as they wanted to look good in the film! I have never taught Anna before and only given one lesson to Julie and her friends a few years ago, so really you are seeing the raw footage. Despite that the lessons go really well and that just goes to show that it really IS easy to teach English and make it fun, and you don't need to be a teacher or have years of training and experience.

The video commentaries will help you understand the process going on in the video. Read the commentary for a section of film and then watch that part of the film. Use the pause button to freeze the video to give you time to read the commentary alongside watching the film. Many useful teaching tips are interspersed throughout the commentaries which may be useful for teachers, but certainly are indispensable reading for parents!

Getting Started

Teachers: If you are a teacher with private pupils already then you will be sufficiently motivated to get straight into the book and my recommendation is for you to pick out three games to use in the next lesson and start like that. Each lesson add in a few more new games and soon your classes will be swinging (if they aren't already!)

Parents: You may be too busy. Or you may feel nervous about starting and put it off. You may spend hours reading every word of this book, reading through all the games and feeling totally overwhelmed as to where to start, as there is so much here. You may be concerned about doing things perfectly and teaching exactly the right thing in the right order, with the perfect accent. Well those things are just excuses not to get started!!

The demo lessons are long because I wanted to fit in as many games as possible to show you. So don't feel you have to have absorbed every game in the book and watched the entire film before you try something out. Little and often is the secret for success so why not watch the first couple of games and play those with your child over a ten-fifteen minute session.

Quite simply take a game like Show Me and take five minutes to play that with your child. There you are, that wasn't so bad! Now take a second game to add to that, and so on.

How Often?

Little and often is the secret if you are a parent, as this will bring the fastest and most enduring results. For parents, if you can do fifteen minutes several times a week your children will build up a substantial vocabulary very quickly and gradually you can add sentences and question forms plus grammar to that.

If you are a private tutor do what you can but do spend at least some time every week with each pupil or the children will just forget what you have been teaching them if they are not exposed to it regularly.

Reviewing what you have already covered is vital, especially with younger children, or the words will go in one ear and out the other. Spend part of each session practising some things you have already learned using revision games and also spend some time introducing new vocabulary.

Remember that children find it boring and pointless to be asked just to repeat words back at you so practise English in the context of a game or a play or a song.

Care with Siblings

Great care has to be taken if you are teaching more than one child in the same session. If you happen to have a younger child who is quicker off the mark than an older child it is best not to share the lesson as the older child may well feel discouraged and decide that he or she does not like English in order to avoid feeling stupid compared to his or her younger sibling. This would be such a shame and the philosophy of these games is to encourage the children and spread love rather than showing one up as insufficient compared to the other.

If the older child is quicker, which is most likely the case, then it is OK to share the lessons as the younger one will not expect to better than his or her older sibling and you can offer plenty of encouragement and have the older one help out the younger one in some of the games.

When playing games with siblings always make them non-competitive, or have the children compete together against you. Competition between siblings can be destructive and is best avoided altogether in this case. Children can accept to have competition at school with classmates but it is not the best thing in a loving home.

What do you teach?

Where do you start? Well so many people think one should start with the alphabet and I just don't agree. I mean put yourself in the shoes of a four year old for a minute and consider what you find more interesting, A,B,C or monkeys, elephants and lions? Letters anyway are abstract and young children prefer concrete objects that they can get their hands on. By all means do teach the alphabet at some point, but it does not need to be the first lesson.

You'll notice from the demo videos that I only do listening and speaking with Anna, who is six, but with Julie, aged 12, we do listening, speaking, reading and writing - in that order. It's my personal preference to start reading and writing from age six, but this is not to lay down the law on the matter, it's just my recommendation.

To start out with complete beginners teach basic vocabulary in themes such as animals, body parts, clothing, toys, professions, furniture, things in nature and so on. Let's say you start out with animals. In the first lesson you might teach three to six animals. In the second lesson you revise those same animals and add some kind of simple grammar such as "What are you?" "I'm a lion" So you play games using those short sentences. Instead of just saying the vocabulary word, you say the sentence.

In the third lesson you add in more animals and continue with that sentence. Depending on your child you may want to add in some descriptive words such a "big lion" and "small cat". It doesn't really matter what you teach as long as it is accurate and you are both enjoying the process. After all it's all English isn't it?

With older children like Julie, who is learning English in school, it's a good idea to follow a structured curriculum. The pace will be a lot faster and you want to build gradually while constantly going back over what you have already covered. If you access a textbook from a local library so much the better, or use the child's school book to pick out our topic. However the textbook is not the main teaching tool, you use it to see WHAT to teach, and do the actual work using the games in this book. Then the child may read the text book for revision once you have taught everything in the unit.

An example of a curriculum is outlined in this book - it is by no means obligatory and is just there as a prop if you need it. It follows a common pattern found in many text books. You are welcome to change the order and dip into it as and when you want to.

What language do you teach in?

Some people feel strongly that teaching should all be in English. I'm pretty flexible on it. The proof is in the pudding however and the truth is that BOTH work just fine!

You may not have any choice in the matter if you are a TEFL teacher working abroad with private pupils and you do not speak the native language. In that case you are obliged to teach exclusively in English, using gestures, pictures and demonstrations to make yourself understood. This is an excellent way to go about things. I personally do use the native language to explain how to play games as I find it saves time and can be extremely useful. However it's perfectly possible to teach without using the native language - you just have to be patient demonstrating how to play a game. Start by teaching useful commands such as touch, stop, give me, point to, sit down, run, stand up, chase, catch so that gradually you can explain more and more games in English, combined with demonstration to make it clear how to play. Consider also introducing the more complex games in stages.

Though I may use the native language (French in the videos) to explain game rules, I use English to say things the children can understand in context - you see me doing this a lot in the videos with Julie. With Anna I say "excellent, good, well done." As you continue to teach the same child over time this "extraneous" vocabulary builds up and more and more of the lesson can be in English, switching as soon as possible to all-English.

Very young children can be alienated by a strange person coming in and jabbering away at them in a language they do not understand. So being able to say something in their tongue can be reassuring.

If you are a parent teaching your own young child, he or she may resist communicating with you using these strange new sounds, especially when the child knows full well that you speak the native language, so it seems quite pointless and even alienating to use English. This is when a friendly puppet comes in handy, who only speaks English, and there is more on this in the teaching twos report that comes with the preschool stories, a good add-on for you as you may follow the stories as a curriculum. Your little puppet is very shy and only comes out when English is spoken. Mummy (or daddy) can translate things the puppet says. The puppet whispers a question into mummy's ear, she translates to the little child, who has to reply back in English.

The idea of making using English a special game also works, so the whole family only speaks English for a given time, such as having an English-only picnic or dinner. If your child resists do not force the use of English. Instead play listening games from this book, he or she will hear and understand the words, then when that is going well gently encourage speaking. Remember that you want to sow the seeds of a JOY of English, languages and learning in general, so forcing a fearful child, (because any resistance is usually fear) to repeat words, or being scornful of poor efforts will back fire, and not only that may have further-reaching negative impact on the child.

Extra ideas at home

Have an English corner at home with books, dictionaries, cassettes, and a noticeboard. The noticeboard could have something new each week - a piece of work, an English label, a photo and a description, a list of new words, a game such as a crossword, or lyrics from a favourite song. Your child or pupil contributes to this board and shows you when he or she adds things.

Do something extra in English once a week: read an English book with your child at bedtime; watch some videos or cartoons in English; let your child listen to a cassette of English songs or nursery rhymes at bedtime, or while you're travelling in the car. The BBC have good children's programmes that you may be able to view online,wherever you are in the world.

Choose a time of the week when everybody in the house speaks English (for example, 10 minutes every Saturday morning as you have breakfast).

While you are out, see how many English words you can find in a shop, supermarket or in the street. Make a list of these words and look them up later with your child.

Use the things you have around you at home. Label objects (10 things in one room each week); put away the shopping in English – ask for each item, your child hunts in the bag and passes it to you. This does lengthen the time it takes you to put the shopping away, but that can be the class for the day. Make cakes together in English – it's a magic cake so it will only taste good if the ingredients hear English spoken during the mixing.

Make picture dictionaries, books, puppets, posters with your child. Display them in your English corner.

Consider finding a pen-friend or e-pal for your child. You can help your child read and write letters or emails. People are absolutely paranoid about perverts in the world today but it's my belief that most people are good, so there is little risk in having a pen-pal, especially if you keep an eye on the correspondence. Bear in mind that having a pen-pal is a two-way process – the other child wants to learn your language too, so share the use of your language and English in the letters/emails. I think letters are better than emails because they are more fun to receive, especially if they have colourful stamps on the envelope and foreign handwriting. That is much more exotic to a child than a printed email.

Use people around you. Can you find English speaking babysitters or au-pairs? Can you create an English library with other parents?

All the above ideas put English in a living context, which is much better than you trying to get your child to repeat a word back to you like a parrot!

Useful additions to this games book

There are stories, plays and songs that go well with these games and which are available as add-on modules. If you have a child who is a beginner in English between the ages of two and a half to five or six then then the 30 preschool stories are an excellent addition to these games.

If you are teaching two year old children there is a special report compiled from interviewing 250 teachers which is included with the first set of preschool stories mentioned above.

For English songs there are three CDs suitable for ages 3 to 8 to play in the car on the way to school or at home. These can be used during lessons in conjunction with the stories or alone.

If you have a beginner to intermediate child aged 4 to 12 then the plays and skits are ideal.

See the **Other resources** section for details.

QUICK START DETAILED INDEX

Step One - Listening games to introduce new language
Step Two - Listening games to consolidate
Step Three - Easy speaking games
Step Four - Consolidating with more demanding speaking games
Step Five - Seeing how words are spelled and Reading
Step Six - Spelling, Writing and English composition games
Games ideal for specific grammar or vocabulary
The Teaching Twos Special Report

It is vital that you play enough listening games for the children to recognise the words well before proceeding to speaking games. If a game is not working observe why not, is it too hard? Are there too many words? Is it too childish or too advanced? Are you going too fast?

Keep it simple and build progressively so that your pupil or child feels confident and enjoys the learning process. If you rush to a speaking or writing game before your pupil has taken the new language or vocabulary on board the game will fail.

Step One Listening games to introduce new words and language

Play as many of these as you need to. Test the water every so often by asking your child to name one of the cards, as is shown in the demo lesson with Anna.

With 3 and 4 year old children, only introduce three words to start with, and play some games just with those three words.

The best games to use very early on during the presentation stage of new vocabulary are:

Bingo
Chanting Game
Delivery Boy
Diving For Treasure
Dressing Up Teddy
Fishing
Hoops or Circles
Hop Bunny Hop
Jump The Line
Matching and Mirroring
Miming Games
Musical Vocabulary
Phoneme Match
Phonemes - Wall Charts
Point and Spin
Rapid Reaction
Roller Ball
Show Me
Tickle Game for Numbers and Alphabet
Using Real Objects
Vocabulary Aim and Throw
What is Hiding in my Pocket?

Step Two More listening games to consolidate new language

Once you have introduced the maximum number of words your group can handle (about 6 new words and 6 you are revising), play more listening games which require a slightly better grip of the words for the game to work well.

These games also allow for fun and effective revision of many words in a short space of time. It is useful to refresh your pupil's memory with a quick listening games before any speaking activity.

Abracadanagram
All Listen
Blind Painter

Colour Wolf
Blind Directions
Grandma's Directions
Directions on the Board
Dress Up Race
Find Me
Go To The Vocab
Grandma's Footsteps Adaptation
Head To Head
Listen
Preposition Obstacles
Pronunciation Hands Up
Recognising Tenses
Run and Touch
Simon says + variants
Spelling and Alphabet Revision
Taboo
The Big Freeze
Traffic Light
True Or False
Twister (+ variant)
Vocabulary Clapping

Step Three - Communicating with the new language

Once your pupil understands the new vocabulary or language structure you are presenting, proceed to some of the speaking games. Here are some good ones to start with:

Action Race
Anagram Time Bomb
Backwards Bull's Eye
Bang The Tin
Blindfold Guessing Game
Boom Chica Boom
Clapping Game
Delivery Boy
Directions on the Board
Duck Duck Goose

Empire State Building

Find The Pairs Memory Game A

Fishing

Getting Warmer

Grandmother's Footsteps Adaptation

Guess The Action

Happy Families

Hidden Picture

Hide And Guess

Hide And Seek Prepositions

Higher Or Lower

Laughing Game

Memory Game (possible step four depending on pupil)

Miming Games

Mystery Bag

Oranges

Phoneme Hangman

Phoneme Match

Phonemes - Wall Charts

Pronunciation Feather Game

Pronunciation: Silent Sounds Game

Question and Answer

Running Race Question and Answer

Sentences

Snap

Sorting

The Crossing

Three Cups

What is Hiding in my Pocket?

What Time Is It Mr Wolf?

Which One Has Gone

Zambezi River

Step Four Consolidating with more demanding speaking games

Balancing Memory Game

Blind Painter

Bogeyman

Brainstorm

Charades

Charades Jeopardy

Don't Drop The Bomb

Dress Up

Dressing Up Teddy

Figure it out

Fizz Buzz

Flash The Cards

Flip A Card

Hangman Additional Variant

Hot Potato

I Spy With My Little Eye

Joker

Keep a Straight Face

Make a Sentence (or a Question)

Making up Stories

Match Up

Name and Chase

Pictionary

Picture Flash Cards

Potato Race

Prepositions

Pronunciation Game

Pronunciation Pictures

Question and Answer

Question and Answer Lottery Match

Question and Answer Treasure Hunt

Russian Roulette

Scissors paper stone

Sentences

Shopaholics

Shopping List Memory Game + Variant

Talking Card Game

Tickle Game for naming vocabulary

Tongue twisters

Treasure Hunt

What Am I?

Whose Shadow Is It?

Who wants to Be a Millionaire Adaptation

Step Five - Reading

Many of the games in steps one to four can be used with word flash cards as well as picture cards. Therefore play a few games using word flash cards in order to familiarise players with spelling. Here are some reading games:

Abracadanagram
Anagram Time Bomb
Backwards Bull's Eye
Bang The Tin
Charades Jeopardy
Delivery Boy
Find The Pairs Memory Game B
Find Me
Go To The Vocab
Fishing
Flash The Cards
Happy Families
Hidden Picture
Higher Or Lower
Jump The Line
Musical Vocabulary
Make a Sentence (or a Question)
Match Up
Name and Chase
Noughts and Crosses
Oranges
Picture Flashcards
Pronunciation Game
Question and Answer Treasure Hunt
Rapid Reaction
Word Flash Cards

Step Six Spelling, Writing and English composition games

Some of these games also involve speaking which is why they come after the listening and speaking games.

Anagrams
Anagram Waddle
Boggle
Guess The Word
Hangman
Make a Sentence (or a Question)
Making up Stories
Mystery Bag
Question and Answer Lottery Match
Remember and Write
Run and Write
Spelling and Alphabet Revision
Spelling Board Game and Variants
Spot the Difference
Write It Up
Writing Race With Worksheet Examples

It should be said that this six-step outline is only a guide. Certainly in my view this is the best order to teach in, however it is flexible. Interchange steps four and five for example, or put step four after steps five and six. What you cannot avoid are steps one to three, in that order, if you want to give your pupil the best chance of being able to use speak and understand English, as opposed to going through the whole of secondary school and retaining virtually nothing, which I can assure you is a common predicament.

Games ideal for specific grammar or vocabulary

99% of the games can be played to learn any grammar or vocabulary. Having said that, certain games are ideal for, but need not be used exclusively for specific language.

Actions: Action Race, Copycat Commands, Matching and Mirroring, Miming Games, Simon Says, Twister, The Big Freeze

Alphabet: Clapping Games, Any of the counting games under the letter C, Hangman, Miming Games, Spelling and Alphabet Revision, Zambezi River

Body parts: Balancing Memory Game, Blind Painter, Copycat Commands, Head to Head, Matching and Mirroring, Simon Says, Twister

Clothing: Colour The Card, Colour Wolf, Copycat Commands, Dress Up, Dress Up Race, Dressing Up Teddy, Simon Says, Twister

Colours: Colour Wolf, Colour The Card, Twister

Comparatives: Higher or Lower

Counting and numbers: See seven games grouped under the letter C. Also Empire State Building and Fizz Buzz

Directions: See four games grouped under the letter D

Families: Happy Families - minimum 2 pupils plus teacher

Prepositions: Hide and Seek Prepositions, Prepositions, Preposition Obstacles

Pronunciation and Phonemes: See the selection of phoneme and pronunciation games under the letter P

Telling the Time: What Time Is It Mr Wolf?

Question and answer games and short dialogues: Bogeyman, Joker, Match Up, Name And Chase, Potato Race, Question And Answer, Question and Answer Lottery Match, Question And Answer Treasure Hunt, Scissors Paper Stone, True Or False, What Am I?

Games ideal for playing with songs or rhymes: Boom Chica Boom, Duck Duck Goose, Hot Potato (minimum 2 pupils), Musical Vocabulary, The Big Freeze.

GAMES A TO B

Use the detailed index above to select games. Watch the online videos and read the written commentary that goes with them to see how to go about things.

Abracadanagram

Category: Listening
Level: All levels
Materials: Pictures, word flashcards or real objects
Age: 4 to 12

How to Play

Julie and I demonstrate this using real objects in the games demo video for "he likes, she likes, it likes, we like, you like, they like" and real objects. This simple use of the game is excellent for the younger ones. With the older ones use word flashcards and more complex sentences.

Give your pupil(s) a set of picture cards of the vocabulary you would like to learn or revise. Say a sentence containing some of the words. Your pupil selects the relevant pictures and puts them in order. For example, with pictures of transport and countries a language option is:

"We went to France by bus". "We went to Italy by plane". Your pupil selects the pictures of the bus and of France in the first example and the pictures of the plane and of Italy in the second example.

Use word flash cards from age 6 upward, or mix up pictures and words. This makes for a more substantial game for the older and more advanced pupils. Once your pupil is ready give out words and pictures for a sentence and let the pupil figure out what the sentence is and put the words and pictures in the right order.

Here's an example to teach "going to". Your pupil knows that "going to" is in the sentence and takes those words out first. He or she then works out the complete sentence using the other words you have given. Examples: "We are going to the beach". "They are going to the circus". "You are going to the beach on Friday". Note that "On Friday you are going to the beach" is also correct.

Language Ideas

Here are ways of adapting the game to suit different levels with the sentence "The cat sat on the mat" as an example:

Young beginners: use only 2 pictures, a cat and a mat.

Up a level: use 2 pictures, a cat and a mat combined with the words 'the, on' and 'sat'.

Up a level: a cat picture and word flashcards for all the other words in the sentence.

For more advanced players still have sentences with clauses in them, such as, "The cat sat on the mat, which was in the hallway, where the dog also slept under the stairs".

Materials

Use flashcards. Picture flashcards help with vocabulary retention. Word flashcards can help with spelling. If you think it is too much work getting material together then simply use word flash cards, which your pupil can write out for you if you like.

Action Race

Category: Easy speaking - repeating words or short phrases
Level: Beginner
Materials: None
Age: 3 to 10
Pace: Wake up

Place two chairs or cushions at the front of the room, one for you and one for your pupil. If you have two pupils they will play each other. If you have three pupils pair up with one of them. Call out an action and the children in the chairs do that action down to the end of the room and back to their seat.

The children repeat "I am jumping" over and over as they complete the action, only stopping when they reach their seats. You may award points for saying the English nicely as well as reaching the seat first. Watch out though for children hurting themselves if playing the game as a race. With the 4 to 6 year old children avoid any kind of competition anyway - all children succeed simply by completing the action and saying the phrase.

Use this to work with any language. Actions are good, such as "I am eating spaghetti", however pupils repeat any given phrase continuously while hopping or jumping down the class. For eight year old children and up tell them they only move when they are speaking and they have to stop if they need to breathe or pause between sentences! Failure to do so means starting at the beginning again.

All Listen!

Category: Listening and Reading Variant
Group size: minimum two pupils
Level: Beginners to Intermediate
Materials: Picture or word flashcards
Age: 4 to 12
Pace: Wake up

How to Play

You need two or more pupils and an empty space for this game. Spread flashcards in a large circle on the floor, with the teacher in the middle. The pupils each choose a flashcard in the circle to stand on. The teacher calls out two of the picture card items. The two players in the circle have to run and stand on those pictures without the person in the middle getting there first. If the player in the middle does get there first then the player who has been beaten goes into the middle. The teacher can continue calling out the vocabulary regardless of where he or she is in the game, or the pupils are ready, they can take a turn calling out the vocabulary.

Language

Either simply name the items on the flashcards, or make sentences. For example if practising food vocabulary call out, "Bananas and milk!" Or use a sentence such as, "I like bananas and milk". The players jump on a picture of either bananas or milk. Both children cannot stand on the milk – one must stand on the bananas. Use any vocabulary you like and any type of question or sentence, practise tenses or any grammar.

Variants

For variety make different patterns of the flashcards on the floor. This will change the game quite a bit. For example with the flashcards in a circle and one player in the middle it is very easy for the player in the middle to jump on a card before the other two. However with the cards in a long line right down the room and the "caller" at one end, it may be very hard for the caller. Play around with different flashcard layouts according to the shape and size of your room and the age of your pupils. Bear in mind not to play for more than ten minutes to keep the game fresh and fun.

Reading variant for age 6 up

Play the game as described above but using short phrases that you write out on cards. For example write out "Hello, how are you?" on one card and "I'm fine, thanks" on another. Write, "Where do you live?" on one card and "I live in India" on another, and so on. For a harder variant cut the sentences or questions in half. Players jump on either the first or second half of the sentence.

Anagram Time Bomb

Category: Reading & Speaking
Level: All levels
Materials: Picture or word flashcards or use the board instead
Age: 6 to 12
Pace: Wake up

Using the target structure and vocabulary write up a series of jumbled questions under letter A with jumbled answers under letter B. For example:

A	B
you how old are?	years am seven old I
name your is what?	Shelley name my is

If you are revising ask your pupil(s) to contribute jumbled questions and answers to the list.

One of you is A and the other B. On the word "go" A works out the question and asks it to B, who works out the answer. A harder variation is to also jumble the vertical order of the lists so that B's answer is not necessarily opposite the corresponding question. Once you have run through the list together at least once and the pupil can do it well swap over so if the pupil was doing the questions he or she now does the answers.

Next produce the "time bomb" device. The ultimate thing here is something that ticks and stops unpredictably. This could be any kind of wind up toy or device, though preferably not too noisy, such as an oven timer or egg timer. Wind up the device and start at the top of the list. The person speaking must hold the device, only passing it on when the sentence is completed. The idea is not to get caught holding the device when it stops. If your pupil hesitates a lot then be nice and don't say your part at a hundred miles and hour before throwing the device back at your pupil. You will have to play this by ear but how you behave can make or break the game. If you have a cheeky child he or she will probably enjoy it if you really do try and go as quickly as possible, but if you have a shy or less confident child, this can make him or her feel threatened. Either way, make sure that you end up with the device at least as often as your pupil. Then the one with the device does a forfeit, such as a silly dance or singing a verse of a song.

While ideal for a question and answer format, nothing stops you from using only questions, or only sentences. If you are drilling a certain structure make the sentences repetitive and stick to the drill initially. When you observe that your pupil is getting the hang of it throw in a few sentences which revise what you have been teaching in recent weeks. Remember for lasting results, not too much new language in any one go, but plenty of revision alongside new elements.

Anagrams

Category: Spelling
Level: Beginners to Advanced

Materials: Sets of letters
Age: 6 to 12
Pace: Calm

How to Play

Cut up the letters of the words you would like to work with and place them in zip lock bags, one word per bag. Stick to very simple words such as CAT and DOG for 6 year old children. In order to make the task of deciphering the word fairly easy give out words which are in the same family of vocabulary, such as food words or professions. A harder option is to give out a clue with every set of letters, which can be written on a sticker on the bag. For the word dog this clue could be "it's an animal" or "woof woof". Now decipher all the words by rearranging the letters in the correct order.

There are various ways to liven this game up:

a. Race your student and give them a head start that is long enough to make it quite close as to who finishes first. The head start could be a certain amount of time, or give yourself three words to do to their one.

b. With two students of equal ability they can race each other. Switch to c. below if you see one child consistently beats the other one.

c. With siblings a collaborative approach is better than introducing competition in the family. Make them work together as a team against you.

A variation is to give each pupil a big pile of letters containing twelve words. Have pictures or clues of the words they must find.

Materials

It's much much more fun to do this with actual letters rather than just pen and paper, because the children can actually move the letters around physically to see how they fit together - a bit like trying different pieces in a puzzle. Scrabble letters are easier to work with and less fiddly than little bits of paper, but make do with what you have. You could make a couple of sets of the alphabet with extra vowels, coloured and laminated, and if you are teaching long term this is a nice option, but not a necessity as you can see from the demo videos with Julie that a few torn up pieces of paper with the letters written quickly on them work just as well.

Anagram Waddle

Category: Spelling
Level: Beginners to Advanced
Materials: Sets of letters
Age: 6 to 12
Pace: Lively

The basis of this game is as described above in Anagrams where pupils figure out words from sets of letters. This is fun packaging for the same task. Place chairs at either end of the room with sets of letters in bags ready for decoding. The teacher starts at one chair and the pupil at the other. On "Go" the teacher has to waddle while the pupil can run to the chair at the other end. Pupil and teacher will cross en route but the pupil should reach his or her chair far before the teacher, who has to do a funny, constricting waddle, which takes a lot longer. This is the head start that the pupil has over the teacher. The pupil and teacher race to make up the word on the chair and call it out when they have deciphered it.

This can be done a single word at a time or there can be five bags with a word in each at each chair and it can be done as a relay where teacher and pupil continue running/waddling to and fro until all the words are deciphered.

With siblings, or with pupils of different levels, let the older students waddle while the younger one runs.

If you are not comfortable doing a silly waddle in front of your pupil(s) then make something up that is quite difficult to do and that you are comfortable with. One method to travel slowly down the room is to take steps where the heel of the front foot must touch the toe of the back foot. This will impede your progress significantly and mean the pupil gets a good head start on you.

As doing the waddle is actually part of the fun it seems a shame for the pupil to miss out, so let him r her do a different type of waddle that is still faster than your one!

Writing variant

Involve the children more by having them make up anagrams for you to decipher as well as the other way around. If you have an older sibling or a better student they can be given this task.

Backwards Bull's Eye

Category: Speaking - making sentences
Level: Beginners to Intermediate
Materials: Something soft to throw and vocabulary pictures
Age: 3 to 12
Pace: Calm

This game involves flying missiles so do it in a clear space, outdoors, or in a room where nothing can be broken. Draw a large target on the board or stick up a circle or piece of paper on a wall or door. Pull out a picture card of some known vocabulary. The pupil thinks of a sentence containing that word. For drilling purposes this sentence can follow a specific structure or tense, such as "I am wearing trousers, I am wearing a skirt, I am wearing shoes". For more advanced pupils and as a fluency and quick thinking task pupils to make up any sentence containing the word, such as, "Those trousers are blue, I like the skirt, I bought some shoes". For children aged three and for a simpler game the pupil just names the word.

If the pupil names the word or makes the sentence up correctly he or she has a chance to aim at the bull's-eye and win a point. To aim children stand with their backs to the target and bend down and aim at the board by looking between their legs. If this is not culturally acceptable for you then modify to suit your needs. For example children may aim by tossing the beanbag over their shoulder without looking at the board, or have children try to hit the target with eyes closed.

If ready the pupil may play the teacher, who misses frequently of course, so the pupil wins or does as well as the teacher.

With siblings of different levels consider having the children work together to name the word or come up with sentences. In that case both children have a go at the bull's-eye simultaneously. Their joint hits are points to add up and compete with the teacher.

Balancing Memory Game

Category: Speaking
Level: Beginners
Materials: Pictures or real items
Age: 3 to 10
Pace: Calm

Place a collection of picture flashcards or objects of vocabulary you would like to revise or practise on the floor or table. Your pupils turns away and closes his or her eyes while you select as many pictures/items as possible and balance them about your body - tucked into your clothing or held between different body parts. One criteria - part of the picture or object must be visible. Your pupil may count to thirty or wait a given time before turning around and taking a look at you.

Option: If your pupil laughs at this point you win a point!

For speaking practice at this point your pupil names each picture, or if you want to work on sentences he or she must say a sentence with the picture word in it. The pupil then turns around and counts again while you change one picture. This time when the pupil turns around he or she has to say which picture is missing.

Swap over! Four year old children will not be able to display pictures as well as older children so give them some ideas beforehand - such as holding picture cards in a fan - as one holds playing cards during a card game - this allows the child to hold up many pictures and make your job of spotting the change much harder.

A game like this will help your child in all subjects because it tones up the brain cells!

Bang the Tin

Category: Speaking
Level: Beginners
Materials: a biscuit lid tin, or saucepan or similar, a spoon or similar - the bigger the better, and picture flashcards
Age: 3 to 10
Pace: Calm

Blindfold the child and give him or her a spoon. Hide a flashcard under the lid of a tin - such as the tin of a biscuit box. The child crawls around banging the floor with the spoon until he or she hits on the tin lid. Remove the blindfold, the child lifts the tin to reveal the flashcard underneath and names it, or makes a sentence using the word depicted. Repeat a few times, moving the tin lid around the room.

I used to play this game before break, so I called it the biscuit game, as once the children had successfully named the flashcard they received a biscuit.

For an effective blindfold I found a Halloween mask in a dressing up shop. Airline eye pads are also excellent. Scarves work but they take longer to put on and can slip down.

Bingo

Category: Listening.
Level: Beginners to Intermediate
Materials: None obligatory or one bingo set per player
Age: 3 to 12
Pace: Calm

How to Play

To play bingo with one student you have to join in. Write down the numbers 1 to 10 on ten pieces of paper and place in a hat or bag. Have each player (including you) write down four numbers between 1 and 10. Pull out a number and call it out. The one with that number on his or her bingo card circles it. Continue until all four numbers are circled. This same version of the game may be used for any numbers – 10, 20, 30, 40 etc. or random numbers between 1 and 100. You could play with all the hundreds (100, 200, 300 to 1000) and all the thousands, even with millions.

Language Ideas

Use the same idea above but using vocabulary words instead of numbers. For example each player writes down four to six professions, or chooses four to six pictures of professions. Take it in turns to draw a picture out of the hat. The player with that profession crosses it off his or her list.

Form sentences with the chosen word to encourage attentive listening. If you are playing Bingo with all new words then I suggest forming sentences with structures your students already know, so that you do not have all new elements. However if you are using Bingo to revise vocabulary, then you might use a new grammatical structure in these sentences so that the pupils hear it repeatedly.

Bingo is a good game to use at the early stage of presenting language as it exposes the players to frequent repetition of the new vocabulary or language. With beginners limit yourself to simply naming the items 'car, dress, pool, mansion'. Build that to include adjectives and specify 'red dress, purple dress, green car'. Expose your players to more vocabulary by being more descriptive, 'beautiful red dress, green sports car', and also expose them to grammatical structures such as 'I wish I had a green car' (players with the green car picture place their item on it), etc.

With young children always play to the end until everyone has completed the bingo card so that everybody "wins."

Materials

Bingo sets are provided with the preschool stories available separately. Otherwise make them with your child by drawing or sticking pictures onto paper or card in a grid.

Bingo with Real Objects

If you have plenty of toys make up pairs of toys, such as two cars, two dolls and so on. Each player takes three toys each and places them on the table. All the other toys go inside a large bag that is not see-through, or box. Take it in turns to reach inside the bag and pull out an item. The player with that same item takes the matching toy and has a pair. The winner is the one who completes all his or her pairs first. If you have plenty of toys use more and make a grid of six to nine toys each to extend the game.

There is a good deal of room for cheating here as players feel around for a toy that they have. A rule could be to pull out the first toy that you touch, to only have two seconds to pull out a toy or you miss your turn, or to hide the toys you are collecting under tea towels and let the other person draw out a toy for you. If you have that toy you bring out the matching pair and display the pair.

Blindfold Guessing Game

Category: Speaking
Level: Beginners to Intermediate
Materials: Objects and a blindfold
Age:3 to 12
Pace: Calm

Blindfold the child. Check with the child if it is OK to be blindfolded. If the child is not keen then allow them to shut their eyes tightly instead although younger children will invariably try to peek! Normally children love to be blindfolded, though perhaps don't do this if it's your first lesson together.

To play you need pairs of objects such as 2 apples, 2 bananas, 2 oranges and 2 pears, plus a box. Let's say the box contains an apple, a banana and 2 pears. The child has to find and name the pears because there are 2 of them, whereas there is only one of everything else. Play repeatedly with the same objects as the child will not know which item is doubled each time.

Fruits are an obvious idea because one can come by them easily, but other ideas are pens, pencils, paper, rubbers, etc. or bathroom items, common kitchen items, or toys. Make sure the items are safe.

Blind Painter

Category: Listening. Speaking
Level: Beginners to Intermediate
Materials: Pen and paper and Blindfold
Age: 4 to 12
Pace: Calm

How to Play

This is like "Pin the Tail on the Donkey". Each painter is blindfolded and draws something such as a face, a house, a person sitting on a chair, an animal, etc. As a listening game tell your pupil what to draw. For speaking practice the painter gives a running commentary while drawing, for example "Here is the head, here are the arms, here are the hands, here is the left leg."

It adds novelty to stick up a big sheet of paper and use fun pens, such as thick fluorescent marker pens, but playing at a table on regular A4 paper is also fine. Be sure to watch that your pupil does not go off the sheet and start drawing on the walls!!

The younger children will find the result very funny while the older children might like the novelty of the game but will tire of it sooner. The teacher and older children may have a go, but with the added difficulty of doing a 360 degree spin on the spot in between each piece of the picture.

Bogeyman

Category: Speaking - ideal for short dialogues

Level: Beginners to Lower Intermediate
Materials: None
Age: 3 to 12
Pace: Excitable

How to Play

Many children really love this game and it's a great excuse for repeated speaking practice of short dialogues. One child has an imaginary bogey on their finger and the aim is to transfer this to the other player. We used to play this as a playground game as children, but if the bogey idea is not appropriate in your culture then use another idea that fits - such as passing on the "Dreaded Lurgy", an imaginary disease where the bubbles stick on your skin when you first get wet!

Rehearse a set mini conversation with your pupil, such as:

Teacher: Hello

Child: Hello

Teacher: How are you?

Child: Fine thanks, and you?

As soon as the child says "and you?" he or she tries to touch the teacher, (metaphorically giving the other player the bogey). Only give a second to transfer the 'bogey'. This time the child starts the dialogue and the teacher will have to try to touch the child. The teacher can of course be somewhat maladroit at this! Also the child can be given longer to try to touch the teacher to make it easier for them. With older children the teachers may well find the pupil is better at the game than they are!

You may use any mini-conversations for this game from asking for a train ticket, to buying something in a store, to ordering in a restaurant, to practising any question and answer routine.

We demonstrate two ways of playing this in the games demo video with Julie.

Boggle

Category: Writing (spelling)
Level: Beginners to Advanced
Materials: Letters or just the class board
Age: From age 6 up. Use short words for ages 6 to 7
Pace: Calm

Materials

Place the letters for a long word or two words, such as "chocolate cake", in a grid on a table top. Allow two minutes for the players to write down as many words as they can find in the given letters. Your student(s) can simply say these to you, or write them down. Count up how many words he or she finds. Give clues, such as "it's an animal that goes meow", to help them find "cat" in "chocolate cake". Needless to say one does not have to make the grid out of a single word. If you want the grid to contain specific vocabulary use those words to make up the grid. Here is an example of a grid with animals.

LOAD
ICCL
OGES
NRTK
BTHB

These 20 letters contain many animal words, such as dog, cat, lion, goat, bat, snake, bird, crocodile, tiger, rat, chicken, horse, hen, cockerel, kitten, toad and maybe some more you will find! Tell the children to think of the animals they know in English, and then look and see if the letters are there.

To help younger students display pictures of the animals in the grid as prompts - the children still have to find the letters in the grid and spell the words correctly. Without the pictures it will be very difficult for most children to find any animals.

Boom Chica Boom

Category: Speaking
Level: Beginners to Lower Intermediate
Materials: None
Age: 3 to 10
Pace: Calm

Thanks go to a teacher for giving me this fun idea. Choose a silly rhythmic phrase and say it together such as: Boom chica boom, I said a boom chica boom, I said a boom chica rocka chica rocka chica boom. At the end of the phrase one of you turns over a flashcard and acts out the picture while the other player attempts to name the word being acted. Repeat the Boom Chica Boom rhyme and swap over so now it's the other player's turn to act.

The game is good for vocabulary revision. Children give a sentence with the word in as well as just naming the word if appropriate. The game also helps fluency and pronunciation by having the children repeatedly using the same rhyme or phrase before the vocabulary acting part. Therefore use a rhyme or nonsense phrase that targets phonemes the children need work with. With French preschool children try this one: Thicker thacker thumper, thicker thaker thump, thicker thacker thicker thacker bump bump bump. French children have difficulty with all those sounds, so even though the words are nonsense it is very useful working on the sounds. One could also use the game idea for meaningful rhymes such as: Act sister act (or brother if it is a boy), do your best. What's on the card? I bet we can guess!

Clapping, finger clicking, foot stamping and other actions during the rhyme add to the fun. The actions could be added in on subsequent playings of the game.

Brainstorm

Category: Speaking
Level: Beginners to Advanced
Materials: None
Age: 6 to adult
Pace: Calm

How to Play

Think of a category of vocabulary that you have previously taught such as professions or daily routine. Set a target number of words your pupil must think of in that category - six words would be quite easy and twelve would be for better or older students. Give each player ten seconds to come up with as many words as possible in the chosen category.

Count up how many words your student finds. After round one show some picture cards as prompts for the category so the pupil remembers more relevant words. Then play again with the same category - the pupil should do better and it's a good excuse to review large amounts of vocabulary quickly. Keep playing with the same category until the pupil reaches the target number of words. If you have a very good pupil you may not need to dwell so much on one category so in that case see if they can do better in the next category.

Examples of categories are cartoon characters, types of transport, musical instruments, animals, types of food, food the pupil likes, food he or she does not like, body parts, clothing items, kitchen items, furniture, actions, toys, jobs, countries, favourite characters, daily routine, what the pupil likes doing at the weekend, subjects at school, and so on.

If you have siblings let them work together to find as many words as possible. One pupil takes the first ten seconds, then the better pupil take the next ten to see what words he or she can add to the list.

By all means give 15 or 20 seconds if you feel that is more appropriate, but always err on the side of not giving enough time to keep up the element of adrenalin and fun. 15 seconds of silence is a long time!

GAMES C TO D

Chanting Game

Category: Very easy speaking
Level: Beginners
Materials: Blindfold
Age: 3 to 10
Pace: Wake up

This is an excellent game for learning vocabulary and to gain confidence by repeating words or short sentences.

Blindfold your pupil and place a picture card or item somewhere in the room. Guide the blindfolded child to the picture by chanting the chosen vocabulary word or short sentence over and over again. Quiet chanting means the child is far away from the picture, louder chanting means the child is approaching the picture. Once the child has found the picture swap over and let the pupil guide you.

If you have siblings take it in turns with the blindfold. This is an opportunity to let the older sibling say a short sentence while the younger child repeats a single word each time.

Charades

Category: Speaking
Level: Intermediate to Advanced

Materials: None
Age: 6 to adult
Pace: Wake up

How to Play

One person mimes a book, a song or a film title by acting out each word or miming the idea expressed in the whole title. Those watching have to guess the book, song or film. The player miming is not allowed to speak at all and starts by indicating if they are miming a book (pretend to hold an open book), a song (pretend to sing), or a film (pretend to hold a movie camera). The other players respond to the mime by calling out the answer, for example, "It's a film" or/and "It's a book". The player miming then specifies how many words are in the title, and the other players respond, for example, "5 words".

The player miming can then either act out the whole title, or choose to act out one of the words, for example he or she might hold up 5 fingers and the audience responds with "fifth word". The actor mimes working in a factory until someone guesses "factory" correctly.

The student miming might then hold up 2 fingers to correspond to the "second word", and indicate that this is "a little word" by holding their thumb and forefinger close together, as if they were holding a small object between them. The audience responds with "a, the, it, an" etc. until someone says "and", which is the correct word in this mime. So far we have "and" and "factory". In this case the book and film is Charlie and the Chocolate Factory. With children of 8 and 9 you might want to think up some good titles for them in advance that are easy to mime in case the children cannot think of any on the spur of the moment.

It's also allowed to mime syllables of words. For example hold up two fingers for the second word, and then place one finger on your forearm to indicate first syllable; two fingers on the forearm indicates the second syllable. Then mime making a pot on a wheel to get the first syllable "pot" of the word Potter for a Harry Potter film.

In addition to syllables one can also mime things that sound like the word. The person miming holds a hand up to his or her ear and the players respond with "sounds like". One might mime carry, which sounds like Harry to get Harry Potter. It's best to play with the basics first and add in these refinements once the children are used to the game.

Charades Jeopardy

Category: Speaking - vocabulary review and grammar practice.
Level: Beginner to Intermediate
Materials: None
Age: 3 to 12
Pace: Wake up

How to Play

Copy a chart onto the board or on paper with vocabulary categories you wish to review. Allocate points for each category, the higher the points the harder the word.

Categories	Point Score			
	100	200	300	400
Animals				
Feelings				
Food				
Jobs				
Score Board				
Team A		Team B		

For each category write out a "mime sheet" with the nouns or words you intend to use and the points they are worth. For example:

Animals	Cat 100 points	Pony 200 points	Fly 300 points	Whale 400 points
Emotions	Happy 100 points	Sad 200 points	Angry 300 points	Satisfied 400 points

Cut up the "mime sheet" and write the category and the number of points on the back of each piece of paper and place face down in a grid. If using the board stick these on with tack. For one on one you might as well use paper and play at a table.

Players take it in turns to select a category and a number of points, such as animals for 200 points, or jobs for 400 points. If your pupils selects "animals for 400 points" you turn that card over, without showing the answer, and you mime the animal to your pupil. If your pupil guesses and names the animal correctly you both win 400 points each. This makes it a collaborative game where the actor really tries to act well and the person guessing does their best to guess. Set yourselves a goal to achieve a certain number of points. Then play again and set a higher goal.

Grammar review

Aside from reviewing vocabulary use this game for sentence or grammar practice. For example the different squares can contain verb tenses such as present tense, present continuous, past continuous and past simple, the past simple being worth the greatest number of points. Students make up a sentence using the correct tense to win the point. Expand this idea for any grammar, any types of sentences or questions. For example to work on questions make each square contain a question word such as: where, why, how, what, which, do, does. A "why question" can be worth 800 points, a "how question" can be worth 400 points, "which" can be worth 300, "where" 200 and "what" 100. Take it in turns to pick a square and make a question starting with that question word. "Why" questions are the hardest to answer usually so avoid this with beginners.

Pronunciation

Use the game also for phonemes or pronunciation. Write out words on the cards and give points according to whether they are easy to say or not. Take it in turns picking a card and let the student say it. If correct award those points to the student.

Clapping Game

Category: Speaking
Level: Beginner to intermediate
Materials: None
Age: 3 to 12
Pace: Calm

Set up a clapping rhythm such as the kind of thing children do in playgrounds. Take it in turns to speak in time to the clapping. This is ideal for practising grammar drills, vocabulary and sentences of any kind. For example take it in turns to describe yourselves or family members in time to the clapping: I've got short brown hair, you've got long curly hair, your mum's got big brown eyes... and so on.

An example of a grammar drill is for the teacher to say a sentence in the present tense which the pupil then echoes back in the past tense. Teacher says: Today I'm going to the beach. The pupil echoes back: Yesterday I went to the beach.

It is quite difficult to think of things to say on the spur of the moment, as in describing members of your family. Julie and I demonstrate this in the games video lesson and we run out of things to say quite quickly! The grammar drill is easier to keep going.

Colour Wolf

Category: Listening or Speaking (colours or articles of clothing)
Level: Beginner
Materials: None
Age: 3 to 10
Pace: Excitable

Thanks to my French nieces for providing this playground game to me. This is a fun version of 'Tag' or 'It'. The wolf shouts out a colour. If you are wearing it you are safe. If you are not wearing it then the wolf can catch you until you find that colour somewhere in the room and touch it. Once you are touching the colour you cannot be caught. Take turns being the wolf with your pupil/s. If your pupil is very young and it is too easy for you to catch him or her then have a rule where you must start on your knees, or do whatever it takes to make it hard for you to catch your pupil. Be aware that with some young children if you catch them they may dissolve into tears and feel that they failed, so in these cases you make sure to never catch them and always let them succeed.

You may do a variant on this game with articles of clothing.

Colour the Card

Category: Speaking
Level: Beginner to Intermediate
Materials: A picture in black and white and the same picture in colour.
Age: 4 to 10
Pace: Calm

How to Play

One player has a coloured picture while the other player has the same picture but in black and white. Player one must not show the coloured picture to player two. Player two has to ask what colour the items are in the picture so that he or she can colour it in. For example if you give girls a picture of a lady in a dress player two can ask questions like: "What colour is her dress, what colour are her shoes, what colour is her hair, what colour is her belt?" Older boys may prefer a picture of a man to colour in. As player one replies "The dress is red, her shoes are white", etc. player two takes the relevant colour and puts a dash of it on the picture, but does not colour the whole thing in at this stage. Once player two has made a note of all the colours the players swap roles. When player one has all the colours down either let the children colour their pictures in all together or they can take them home and do it later if they feel like it. You certainly do not want to spend much precious class time colouring. You can always compromise and let pupils colour for a few minutes and then tell them to finish it in their own time.

Materials

For materials find and print clip art in black and white. Have the children colour one version, but keep the other in black and white. To avoid the colouring step it's possible to print coloured clip art in 'greyscale' and print one version in grey and the other in colour.

A way round the problem of finding or creating pairs of pictures is to give out black and white pictures to both children. The children themselves then take it in turns to decide what colour the items in the picture will be.

Copycat Commands

Category: Listening

Level: Beginner to Intermediate
Materials: None
Age: 4 to 12
Pace: Wake up

How to Play

This is an extremely simple game where you tell your pupil to do certain actions while miming them and they copy you. It is good for the initial introduction of vocabulary and also for a quick revision of vocabulary before a game such as Simon Says. As your pupil becomes familiar with the language stop miming and just give the commands.

Here are some things your pupil might mime, to give you ideas to add to: Dance / Jump / Run on the spot / touch your nose / touch any body part / touch a colour / touch an item of clothing / touch a friend's leg, arm, etc. / open a book / pick up a pen / fold a piece of paper / pass the paper to a neighbour / screw up the paper / throw it at someone! / Pick it up / unfold it / write you name on it / be silent / crouch down / mime a chicken / write the number 7 / sing do re mi / tap your feet / clap your hands once / clap your hands five times / stand up / sit down / stand up if you're wearing a skirt / sit down if you are wearing shoes / stand up if you like tennis / sit down if you like chocolate / be a Jedi knight / Girls: be a princess / boys: be a prince / fly a plane / touch your nose if you like chocolate / say 'hello' if you have a sister.

Counting and Number Games

Add up the Dice

Speaking, ages 6 upwards

Roll three dice and have your pupil add up the total.
To do the higher numbers say that each number on the dice is x10 or x100 its face value, so 6 would become 60 or 600.

Clap and Count

Speaking, all ages

Clap or bang a number of times and have your pupil call out how many times you clapped. If you have two children have them play with each other. With younger children clap slower so they can follow you, and with the older ones make it quite difficult by clapping as fast as you can.

Count the Cards

Listening, all ages

Give out 10 to 20 cards to each player, this includes you if you have one pupil. The players count out as fast as possible the number you tell them. You say something along the lines of, "On your marks, get set, 3!" And then you and your pupil race to count out three cards, sit on your hands when finished and say "3!" Even if you manage to count out the cards faster than your pupil you might take longer to sit on your hands and this allows the pupil to finish before you quite realistically.

You won't want to make it a race for the 4 year old children, but just have them count out the cards in their own time. With siblings, if the same child keeps winning all the time have him or her take turns to call out the numbers,or put the siblings in a team against you.

Guess the Price

Speaking, all ages

Find three pictures of sofas in catalogues or magazines. Take the description from the magazine or write one and give each item a price - preferably the real price. Show the pictures and describe the sofas to your pupil and then read out the three prices. Your pupil must try to match the price with the item. This is a good listening comprehension task. If you take real descriptions from catalogues, or write them it can be a reading comprehension task. Once you have done it once or twice with your student let him or her prepare some items for you to guess the price of.

The items can also be totally fictional where you make them up and use no pictures, which would work for older pupils. For younger pupils use real objects such as fruits or toys you may have at home. Put out three toys on the table. Describe each toy using language appropriate to the level of your pupil - such as "he's an astronaut and he's in a grey space suit". Then give the three prices and let the pupils match the price to the item.

How Many?

Place a number of items around the room at "Guessing Stations", or place them all on your table. Your pupil visits each guessing station and either counts or attempts to guess how many items there are at each station. Use things such as:

A jar of coins
A jar of sweets
A bag of small objects
A see-through bag of biscuits
A see-through bag of peanuts
A pile of magazines
A pile of papers
A page full of words
A pack of envelopes

Give a time frame for the task to add an element of excitement for players over about age 7. Then when your pupil has all the answers written down come back together and ask how many coins there are in the jar - or first guessing station item. Your pupil gives you the answer and you say if it is higher or lower. The pupil makes another guess right there and you say if it is higher or lower. Continue through the items and then let the pupil go round the guessing stations again to make a more accurate guess based on your information. Come together again and let the student give you the answers again. This allows you to do numbers in isolation - and also "more than or less than" or "higher and lower".

With young children have piles of a few objects only so pupils count them up physically. Use the ideas in the list above for older children. Needless to say any counting is to be done out loud in English, or the answer doesn't count.

Match Stick Game

Speaking, age six upwards

This is best with a minimum of three players. It can be played with only you and one child but not for as long as it is considerably less interesting. It's best played with a child who can already do rudimentary arithmetic but that said even a four year old may play the game just guessing randomly and without trying to do any sums.

This is the classic game where a group of people each have 3 matches each or similar items behind their backs. Sitting round in a circle, each player takes between 0 and 3 matches and hides them in their fist. All players hold out one fist in the centre of the circle, the object being to guess the total number of matches in all the hands. Each player takes a guess. If someone says 6, no one else can say 6 in that round. Aside from numbers this game can also be used with "I think there are", "There are", "I believe there are".

Pass the Ball

Speaking, all ages

To learn to count from 0 to 20, throw a ball back and forth or round in a circle counting in unison with each throw. When the players become good at counting have only the player throwing the ball say the number. The 4-5 year old children roll the ball across the floor instead of throwing it if preferred.

You don't always have to start from 0 if you want to do higher numbers. Count up in tens: 10 20 30 40 50 etc. Or count up in 2s: 2 4 6 8 10 12 and so on, or in 3s: 3 6 9 12 15 etc. Or count all numbers with a 9 in them: 9 19 29 39 49 59 69 79 89 91 92 93 etc. Use this game for the alphabet too.

When your pupil becomes good at this, whistle or clap to signal a change in direction so they count down instead of up. This allows you to repeatedly count over a "sticky" area and reinforce those numbers by counting them several times in the context of the game.

See also Fizz Buzz, Don't Drop the Bomb and Higher or Lower.

Delivery Boy

Category: Listening and Speaking
Level: Beginner to Lower Intermediate
Materials: 3 small boxes such as tissue boxes or shoe boxes. Picture flashcards.
Age: 3 to 9
Pace: Wake up

Take 3 empty tissue boxes and stick one or two pictures on each box. If you do not have tissue boxes use any kind of box (or use envelopes) and cut a slot into it so that it is like a post box. You could stick the flashcards to the box, but if you want to reuse the boxes for the same game but with different vocabulary another time then just lay the pictures out behind each box. Scatter the boxes about the room, or if you have several rooms you could put a box in each, leaving the doors held open.

Start with a stack of replica flashcards of the ones you have put out by the boxes. The child takes a picture from you, names it and goes off to find the correct box. Or for a listening version, tell each child which picture to take from the selection you lay out. On finding the box with the same picture the child posts the picture in the slot of the box.

The child then runs back to you for another picture. To encourage speaking the child may name the picture you give in order to have the chance to go and post it. If you are practising sentences then the child says the sentence with the word in before going off to post the picture.

At the end the child brings you the three boxes and you both count out the contents of each box, or name the pictures as you pull them out.

Diving for Treasure

Category: Listening
Level: Beginner to Lower Intermediate
Materials: Pictures or objects
Age: 3 to 10
Pace: Wake up

I got the idea for this game from my nephew Archie, when he was 8.

Tell your children that they are pirates who are looking for treasure. They dive down to the bottom of the sea and pick up the treasure they find there. Before they go they take a big breath in, swim down to the sea floor holding their breath until they come up with the treasure. In fact all they are going to do is go and pick a picture up off the floor!

To prepare, lay out a whole selection of pictures of vocabulary you have already introduced your pupil to. The child dives and fetches the treasure which you name. Each time the child must come back with the correct picture. In the video lesson with Anna I said she had to save the animals at the bottom of the ocean and she had to get the right one or the animal could drown. It was very easy for her to do this in one breath so we expanded the distance she had to run to make it more fun.

To turn ordinary words into treasure say that they are magic, which is why they can live at the bottom of the sea; a magic book, a magic pencil, a magic pony, etc.

If you have no flashcards but do have pictures on the wall, or real objects then the children can swim over to the right picture, touch it to show you they know what treasure they are looking for, and then dive down to fetch it and bring back an imaginary item.

3 Games for Directions

Blind Directions

Category: Listening and Speaking
Level: Beginner to Intermediate
Materials: Blindfolds
Age: 4 to 12
Pace: Wake up

Lay out a course to follow in an open space in the house, classroom or garden. Create this by placing books or flashcards on the floor between the start line and the finish line.

Player A blindfolds player B who stands on the starting line. Now player A directs player B through the obstacle course you have created to the end and back. Use directions such as: "Go straight on. Stop. Go left. Go right". Complicate the vocabulary used as the level of your pupil evolves. Four year old children may not know the difference between left and right in which case play simply with go, stop and turn towards me or away from me.

Then swap over and let the pupil direct you.

With young children this will be enough. With older ones time each other and see who can guide the person the fastest, or let the pupil have several turns at being guided and see if he or she can do it quicker each time.

Materials

For a blindfold airline eye pads work best, as you do not waste time tying them up the way you do with a scarf. You may also find children's masks in dressing up shops or supermarkets at Halloween, and tape over the eye holes.

Grandma's Directions

Category: Giving Directions and general listening
Level: Beginner
Materials: None, space helpful
Age: 4 to 12
Pace: Wake up

This is a version of Grandmother's Footsteps. You are Grandma standing with your back to the room. Grandma calls out directions such as: "left, turn left, go left, right, go straight on, go backwards, go forwards, stop". Add adverbs or details to these commands, such as quickly, on one foot, angrily.

At any moment Grandma suddenly turns round. Your pupil must instantly freeze and if Grandma sees anyone moving that person takes Grandma's place or goes back to the start. Your pupil has to make it to Grandma to finish. Swap over and let your pupil have a chance at being Grandma. It's possible to make the task much much harder for older children by having them hop angrily on one foot, then turn round – they will be moving!

Directions on the Board

Category: Listening or speaking - Giving Directions
Level: Beginner
Materials: Big piece of paper or board to draw on
Age: 3 to 12
Pace: Wake up

In this game you will guide your pupil to draw something - the fun part is that your pupil will be wearing a blindfold and will not know what is being drawn until the end when the blindfold is removed. Pick an object that is easy to draw such as a house, an animal or a piece of furniture - avoid making the drawing too complicated or it will not work.

You pupil holds the pen over the board or large piece of paper. You say "down" and the pupil lowers the pen to make contact with the board or paper. You say, "left" - the pupil starts drawing a line to the left until you say "stop". And so on. You will have previously taught the commands that you need such as left, right, up, down, lift (to lift the pen up from the paper and move it in the air to where you need it). Use any other games such as copycat commands or Simon Says to teach those words first.

Get ideas for what to draw from simple colouring books or objects in your house.

In a future session for revision, let your pupil guide you to draw something for speaking practice.

Don't drop the Bomb

Category: Speaking - counting 0-20 or in tens or 100s, or the alphabet
Level: Beginners
Materials: None
Age: 5 to 12
Pace: Wake up

Take it in turns tapping a balloon in the air - with younger children you need as large a balloon as possible otherwise they do not manage to hit the balloon high enough or keep it airborne. Each time someone taps the balloon everyone counts and you aim to tap the balloon ten times and reach ten. When you are good at that count backwards or count up in tens or twos or threes to use more numbers.

The "bomb" part of this game is that the balloon is not allowed to touch the floor - if it does it explodes. This only works with older children as the younger ones sometimes feel that the bomb going off is failure and they don't seem to like the concept.

If you are playing with siblings and you have an older one who hogs the balloon and will not share the tapping make a rule where one may only tap three times in a row, after that it must be a different person who taps the balloon.

Dress Up

Category: Speaking
Level: Beginner to Intermediate
Materials: Clothing and accessories such as belts, hats or scarves
Age: 4 to 12

Pace: Wake up

How to Play

This game is for revision of clothing but not for learning it initially. Play Dress Up Race below beforehand as preparation. Your pupil starts by dressing up in another room, or without you looking. Use adult clothes which are easy to put on or contents from a dressing up box. When your pupil is ready you have one minute to memorise what he or she is wearing. If you have siblings they can dress up together and you must memorise both outfits.

Now give one minute to your pupil to change one or more items. Then you look again and say what items have changed. If scoring, give a point for each correct change noted. Some examples of language are:

Simplest: Point to the item that has changed and say "the hat" or "black hat"

Harder: You took the hat off. You put on a shirt. You put on a pink shirt

Possessives: Elisa is now wearing John's hat

Present and past continuous: Elisa is wearing the black hat and before she was wearing the pink skirt

Then swap over the roles. Make the changes obvious with a four or five year old so it is easy for them to spot!

Materials

If you have a dressing up box use it - pre-teach the items using other games first of course. Girls love long fluffy scarves made out of fake feathers, shawls, extravagant skirts and hats, boys love cowboy hats, gun holsters, waistcoats, Mexican hats, etc. If you are pushed for time just use a few different coloured hats and scarves. You might even use the children's own hats if it's winter and you are in a cold country. Using adult clothing is fun as the children always enjoy dressing up in oversized items, they look funny in them and they are quicker to put on and off. Avoid anything that is slow to put on like tights or a ballet dress as you will spend the whole time getting changed - although in a parent/child situation that can be a fun way to spend time together.

Boys will probably not like dressing up in girls' clothes, but if you are a male teacher your pupil may well find it hilarious if YOU put on a female item! If you are taking private pupils make sure this kind of messing about is acceptable in the culture you are teaching in - if in doubt check with the parents first to see if they are OK with it. You don't want to lose a pupil because parents think you are perverted!

Dress Up Race

Category: Listening
Level: Beginner
Materials: Clothing and accessories
Age: 4 to 12
Pace: Wake up

This is a game to use to teach clothing before playing a game like Dress Up (above). Play Jump the Line first to introduce the clothes, followed by a game like Bingo. Next place a pile of clothes and accessories at the end of the room. If teaching clothing for the first time stick to a maximum of six new items. By all means place several of the same item in the pile of clothes to make a bigger pile. You and your pupil stand at the other end of the room. You now name a clothing item which is the signal to race off down to the pile of clothes, grab the item, put it on and race back to the start line. Do this as a race or just do it together in a relaxed way for fun. Playing some music in the background can also be fun.

Be sure to let your pupil have a good head start on you - or alternatively feel free to fumble putting the clothes on. Of course one does not have to bother with doing buttons up and so on.

Dressing Up Teddy

Category: Listening Idea and Speaking Role-Play
Level: Beginners and up
Materials: Dolls, teddies or toys that have clothes or accessories
Age: 4 to 12
Pace: Calm

Thanks to a preschool teacher for giving me this excellent game idea for clothing.

Listening Dressing Game

Arrange for your pupil to bring in several dressed dolls or teddies. Start by undressing the dolls/teddies and put all the clothes into a pile on the floor or table. Next line up the teddies in order. Now describe an item your pupil should put on the first toy, such as a pink skirt. The next clothing item goes on the second toy and so on.

The children love it, especially when things are too large or too small for a certain doll, when a pullover only dangles down from one arm.

Speaking Role-Play

This game can be changed slightly into many other versions such as just letting pupils sort the clothes into piles of different colours or playing shop with like a little role play where the toys are customers and your pupil is the shop assistant. The toys (you do the voices for this) ask to try on different items, say please, thank you. Your pupil says "here you are" when handing the toys clothing items, and "you are welcome" when you say thank you". The golden rule is to keep it simple and only add in more language once your pupil has a grip on the basics, that way you have a more fluid role-play and consequently one that is more fun to do.

Duck Duck Goose

Category: Speaking
Level: Beginner
Materials: Any four items to mark four spots on the floor
Age: 4 to 10
Pace: Wake up

This game is excellent for practising new vocabulary and for revision. It involves repeating words or short sentences over and over again, thus really drilling them in while playing a fun game.

How to Play

Place four chairs in a circle. If chairs are not convenient use cushions or failing that use any four items such as books or pieces of paper to serve as "markers". Your pupil sits on one of the chairs or "markers". Start behind your pupil, say "duck" and walk around the circle to the next chair, where you say "duck" again, continue to the third chair and say "goose". Go to the fourth chair and say "duck", continue to the chair where your pupil is sitting and say "duck" again, at the next chair say "goose". Continue like this the third time round the "duck, duck, goose" you will find yourself back at your pupil's chair. When you pronounce "goose" this time your pupil jumps out of the chair and into the next chair along. You try to sit down in your pupil's chair before your pupil manages to sit down in the next door chair. It should be very close - especially if your pupil anticipates you saying "goose", which is very likely to happen once he or she understands the game!

If you sit down before your pupil then it is your pupil's turn to walk round the circle. If you start in a different place in the circle each time the final "goose" will fall differently. Add an extra chair if you play with siblings.

When your pupil is ready, change the vocabulary, for example, sticking to the animal theme use tiger, tiger, snake! Cow, cow, pig! Play with short sentences such as "I like pizza, I like pizza, I like cake."

GAMES E TO G

Empire State Building

Category: Speaking
Level: Beginner to Lower Intermediate
Materials: building blocks or any items that can be stacked on top of each other but which topple over after a while. We used to do this with packs of cards and build a card tower but today's playing cards seem to be flimsy and useless compared to ones we had as children. Try a variety of items such as a book, a pencil, a rubber, a piece of paper etc. Use anything that could be interesting to stack.
Age: 3 to 12
Pace: Calm

Take it in turns to stack your bricks, cards or items on top of each other to make the Empire State Building, or any other tall building that has relevance to you such as the Eiffel Tower, Big Ben, the Leaning Tower of Pisa or whatever the tallest building in the world is right now.

The most obvious language idea to use with this game is counting. Each time a child places a brick on the tower count up the next number. However naming the item you are placing or naming any word in English is a good way to practise vocabulary. For example in order to be allowed to place your brick or item you must first name a picture, or make a sentence up.

So for three year old children keep it simple where they simply name a picture or touch the correct picture or object that you name, and then place the brick on the tower. For older children who are more advanced they turn over a flashcard from a pile and make up a sentence with that word in it. Or give them a theme such as clothing and they must think of an item of clothing before being able to play. For revision have the pupil think up five items of clothing before being able to place the brick. In the next round he or she thinks up five colours and so on. Take it in turns - the pupil can give you themes where you think up words too.

Figure It Out

Category: General language or specific vocabulary revision
Level: Beginner to Intermediate
Materials: Sets of clues - either written or in pictures
Age: 6 to 12
Pace: Calm

Prepare sets of picture cards or write out sets of words (if you want to revise spelling). Each set is to represent a theme or place. Mix in some real items if you have them to hand.

With younger children do not be complex, for example a Cinderella theme would be a glass slipper, a pumpkin, a couple of ugly sisters, a princess, a prince, and a ball. A beach would be sand, water, sunglasses, sun tan oil, a sand castle, etc. For the older ones be a little more cryptic, for example:
Chocolate cake: chocolate, flour, butter, cake decoration, and candles
Police station: policeman, handcuffs, key, parking ticket
Hairdressers: hairbrush, scissors, money, mirror
So with your words or sets of pictures or items dispersed about the class give a 1-minute time limit at each set for your student(s) to guess the theme or keyword, which they write down, or tell you when they have figured it out. Then let your pupils make up clues for you to guess.

Find Me

Category: Listening
Level: Beginner to Lower Intermediate
Materials: Classroom items or any items you have to hand
Age: 3 to 12
Pace: Wake up

Stage One

Similar to Copycat commands this is a simple game where the players show their understanding of vocabulary and it is a good game for introducing new vocabulary or revising it before a speaking game. Very simply you ask the players to show you an item. For example you say, "show me a pen" and pupils point to or hold up a pen. "Show me a blue pen" and students hold up a blue pen. Here are other ideas: show me the floor, the ceiling, the wall, the left wall, the right wall, a rubber, a ruler, a friend, a girl, a boy, a hand, a leg, a friend's foot, a blue skirt, a sock, a door, a pen in a pencil case, a pen under a pencil case and so on for the prepositions, etc.

The items can be on the walls, on picture cards spread about the room, semi-hidden, or real objects scattered about, again partially hidden.

Stage Two

Give the command, "find me a pen". Count out loud up to five. The pupil must have found a pen, or a picture of a pen by the time you reach five. If successful your student keeps the pen/picture as a point. See how many points he or she can earn from ten commands. Swap over and let your pupil hide the items and ask you to find them. See this demonstrated in the lesson with Anna. Notice how I slow the counting down when she brings back the wrong picture so he has time to bring me the correct one.

Alternatively play music and see how many pictures the pupil can find and bring to you before the end of the song.

If you have two pupils they can race each other - either by having only one picture at the end so only one pupil will return with a picture, or by having two piles so they will both return with a picture, but one will cross the line first.

With older children if you make it too easy so they succeed every time they will most likely not find the game as much fun. Keen observation of your pupil during the game will give you an indication of how to play it.

Find the Pairs Memory Game A

Category: Speaking
Level: Beginner to Intermediate
Materials: 2 matching sets of picture or word cards or a mix of both
Age: 4 to 12
Pace: Calm

How to Play

Take two sets of identical pictures, shuffle them and spread them out face down. The card must not be see-through and placing the pictures on a white surface helps with this somewhat. The pictures can be laid out randomly or in a grid. Player A turns over two cards and names the items. If they are a pair player A keeps the cards. If they are not a pair player A turns them back over, leaving them face down in the same place. Player B now turns over two cards, attempting to turn over two identical pictures, and naming the items. The game continues until all the pairs have been found.

The younger the players the fewer pairs you lay out initially. In the classic game when a player turns over a pair he or she gets another go. However as the goal is to practise language rather than find a winner, it is preferable to let each person have only one turn. This makes it less likely for the brighter person to win all the pairs leaving the others with nothing. An ideal way to even up the game with siblings or if it is just you and your child or pupil playing is to give your the weaker/younger player two turns while other players have only one.

Language Ideas

The language possibilities to use with this game are endless, keeping an eye as always on the complexity, so that the game does not drag.
Vocabulary: Each player simply names the item on the card.

Phrases: Each player forms a short phrase including the item on the card. For example with pictures of people one could use adjectives such as "a pretty girl", "a tall boy", or with places "a big city", "a small village".

Sentences: Each player forms a sentence using one or both of the items. For example if you are using pictures of food players can say: "I like butter and milk", or "I like butter but I don't like milk". If you are using pictures of people players can say; "Her name is Claudia" or "She is a dentist", or "She is from Spain", or "She is wearing trousers", etc. One can also work with comparatives such as "the girl is taller than the boy", or "the girl is older than the baby". More advanced students can do more complicated structures, depending on the language you would like them to use. For example, "I was going to buy some milk but I bought some cheese instead", or "I have never been to London but I have been to Paris".

Questions: Players can ask questions related to each picture they turn over. For example with sets of people one can ask, "What's her name?" Or "Where does she live?" or "How old is she?"

Find the Pairs Memory Game B

Category: Reading and speaking
Level: Beginner to Intermediate
Materials: Two matching sets of word flash cards
Age: 6 to 12
Pace: Calm

To be played in the same way as Find the pairs memory game A, using word flash cards instead of pictures, for reading and frequent exposure to spelling. Make up phrases, sentences and questions in exactly the same way with these words as with the pictures, as described above.

Fishing

Category: Listening or speaking
Level: Beginner to Lower Intermediate
Materials: drinking straws and small pictures on normal paper
Age: 3 to 12
Pace: Calm

The game consists of sucking in through a drinking straw and attempting to pick up a small piece of paper, holding that paper on the end of the straw and crawling across the floor to a designated finish point a metre or two away. At first your child may not be able to do it. In the lesson with Anna she takes some time to figure it out. At first she thinks you blow on the paper to move it, and that's an easier variant for use with children aged three.

If your child really cannot do it after five minutes of trying – because children will usually be keen to keep trying! - tell him or her to keep the paper pictures and the straw and practise later, and that you'll play again in the next session.

For listening skills tell the children which picture to fish out, and for speaking the children can name the pictures they manage to bring back.

Incidentally this is a good game to quiet a child down, as it requires concentration and one can't speak while sucking through a straw!

Fizz Buzz

Category: Speaking
Level: Beginner to Intermediate
Materials: None
Age: 6 to adult
Pace: Wake up

The first player says one, the next says two, the first player (or third one) says three, and so on. Run through some numbers like this for practice. Now add in an element; every time the number 2 comes up, or a number with 2 in it (such as 12, 20, 22, 26, etc.), the player says FIZZ instead of the number. For example: 1 FIZZ 3 4 5 6 7 8 9 10 11 FIZZ 13 14 15 16 17 18 19 FIZZ FIZZ FIZZ etc. until 30, then 31, FIZZ, 33 etc.

Once your pupil has mastered this idea to some degree throw in another element, such as any number with a 5 in it becomes BUZZ. This would give: 1 FIZZ 3 4 BUZZ 6 7 8 9 10 11 FIZZ 13 14 BUZZ 16 etc.

Now if you want to make things really complicated, say that any number which is divisible by 2 is a FIZZ BUZZ. For example: 1 FIZZ 3 FIZZBUZZ BUZZ FIZZBUZZ 7 FIZZBUZZ 9 FIZZBUZZ 11 FIZZ 13 FIZZBUZZ BUZZ FIZZBUZZ etc.

However this would be for older children and adults only or it would be too complicated to be fun. For an easier version make the FIZZ BUZZ any number with a three in it.

Other language ideas

This fun game also works with vocabulary. Here is an example: Using animal vocabulary any animal ending in an R is followed by FIZZ, and any animal ending in a T is followed by BUZZ, any animal ending in an E is followed by FIZZ BUZZ. A round might look like this:

Tiger, FIZZ, Antelope, FIZZ BUZZ, Elephant, BUZZ, ant, BUZZ, Lion, duck, bird, crocodile, FIZZ BUZZ, etc.

This game is quite tricky and is better for age 8 upwards. You would definitely want to precede the game with a game like Brainstorm, or Ping-pong beforehand to refresh everyone's memory of animal vocabulary. To make the game easier spread picture cards of animals for the above example, or of the relevant vocabulary, out on the table or floor to act as prompts and help the flow of the game.

Flash the Cards

Category: Speaking
Level: Beginner to Intermediate
Materials: Picture flashcards and something to hide them under.
Age: 3 to 12
Pace: Calm

This is a vocabulary revision game. Collect a selection of pictures of words you would like to revise. Lay the pictures out face down in a grid or circle. Add mystery by placing an object on top of each card. The object of the game is for the children to identify each picture until the whole grid or circle is uncovered and all the picture cards revealed.

Ask the child to get ready, ready, steady, and GO! Whoosh one of the flashcards rapidly in front of the child, hopefully giving them just enough time to catch a glimpse of it. If the child identifies the picture he or she can name it. If he or she cannot name it ask what colour it was and then whoosh it past the child again, a little slower but still not too slowly. Once a picture has been named it is placed back on the floor or board picture side up.

With older children let them also take turns whooshing the cards in front of you and see who can win the most cards. This game is more challenging if you use pictures that have not been used before. Shopping catalogues are excellent for pictures of common vocabulary items – at least you get some use out of them instead of them going straight into the recycle bin!

Flip a Card & Variants

Category: Speaking
Level: Beginner to Intermediate
Materials: Playing cards
Age: 6 to adult
Pace: Calm

This game is good for vocabulary revision and sentence construction. Assign two letters of the alphabet for each playing card and write this up. For example the Ace stands for letters A and B, for, letters C and D, 3 is for letters E and F; continue and you will find that the King corresponds to the letters Y an Z. There are 13 playing cards and 26 letters of the alphabet so each card will correspond to two letters.

Shuffle the deck of playing cards and place it face down in a pile on the table or floor. The first player turns over a card and says a word that starts with one of the two letters assigned to it. So if you turn over a 4 of hearts you think of any word starting with the letter G or H. If successful the student keeps that card as a point. Continue playing until there are no more cards in the deck.

Collaborative variant: If you have siblings play as a collaborative game with your two children/pupils forming a team against you. Within given time limit students endeavour to win as many cards as possible from the deck. Then you have a go - and of course you sometimes find it hard to think of something!

Intermediate Variant: Here students turn over several cards and say or write down a sentence using words beginning with the given letters. This sentence construction may be done rigidly following a given grammatical structure or it may be used for general language.

For example a student turns over three playing cards, which correspond to the letters A or B, G or H and S or T. If required to use the past simple tense with these letter options examples are: Adam hated soccer, or, Beth got a tie. If allowed to make up any sentence freely examples are: Aunty goes shopping. Bridget has teeth.

For variations allow extra words to be added in the sentence to allow the students to be more creative. One may also choose to allow the words starting with the 'playing card' letters to be placed in the sentence in any order.

Forfeits

Below are ideas for forfeits that can be used in many games. Giving a forfeit is not a punishment but a useful way to make a game fun and you will find reference to forfeits within certain game descriptions.

Here are some ideas for forfeits below:

Name a picture flashcard

Make a sentence or a question using the target language

Ask a friend any question in English

Name three things you like

Answer a question the teacher asks such as, Do you have a sister?

Hold an orange under your chin and pass it to a neighbour

Walk about holding an orange under your chin

Walk about with an orange between your knees

Balance a ball on your head for three seconds

Bounce a ball ten times and count to ten

Or bounce a ball saying 10, 20, 30 etc. up to 100

Say your name backwards. (You may need to write this out.)

Write your name in the air with a body part such as your head or your elbow, or even your bottom! (If acceptable in your culture of course).

Do a silly dance or sing a song

Pretend to be a chicken, pig, dog, cat, lion, tiger, snake etc.

Count to 10

Yawn until you make someone else yawn

Do a sum such as 70 minus 60

Pretend to be a model and walk the catwalk

Pretend to be Spiderman or batman

Fight and be killed by Darth Vader with your light sabre

Hop round the room holding one foot with your hand

Pretend to be a dying fly

Doggy actions such as wag your tail, beg, bark

Say a tongue twister (see Tongue Twisters for ideas)

Do a roley poley (a forward roll)

Make someone laugh

Limbo under a stick

Walk across the room on your knees

Stand on one leg and do not smile for ten seconds

Try and make someone else laugh in ten seconds

Pull a funny face

Buzz like bees to see who buzzes the longest without taking a breath

Look at someone and do not smile for a full minute

Say a sentence about kangaroos, or elephants, or any other topic

Intermediates say 2 or 3 sentences about a topic

Advanced students give a one-minute spontaneous talk about a topic

Ask your pupil to ask friends at school to come up with funny forfeits for homework – you'll gets lots of great ideas that appeal to your student's age level – collect them in and add them to your list for future use in the games

Getting Warmer

Category: Speaking
Level: Beginner
Materials: Pictures or objects to search for
Age: 3 to 10
Pace: Wake up

Your pupil hides an object or a flashcard. You then search for it. Your pupil guides you by telling you if you are getting close. When you are far away you are cold. As you get nearer you become warm and eventually hot, or burning! Use cold, warm and hot, or getting warmer, getting colder, getting hotter, very very hot!!! To work with other vocabulary, tell the children to use other words to signify getting further away or coming closer. Milkshake could signify moving away and pizza could mean coming near.

In the lesson with Anna where we are looking for hidden flashcards she starts doing this in French on her own initiative. In the next lesson I would teach her how to say hot and cold and play again, but with the clues in English.

Go to the Vocab

Category: Listening or Speaking - giving commands and naming vocabulary
Level: Beginner to Lower Intermediate
Materials: None
Age: 3 to 10
Pace: Wake up

Lay out a course of pictures or objects on the floor of the vocabulary you would like to use. Have a matching set of pictures or words in a hat. For the listening version while your pupil is learning to recognise the words pull a word or picture out of the hat and tell him or her to go to that object or picture in the course. Continue to pull all the words out of the hat until it is empty. To include more vocabulary vary the action verbs you use such as "hop to the pencil", "run to the hat".

When your pupil is ready let him or her tell you which picture to go to. This can be done during another lesson so you do not kill the game by playing it for too long.

Grandmother's Footsteps Adaptation

Category: Listening or Speaking
Level: Beginner to Intermediate
Materials: None
Age: 3 to 12
Pace: Wake up

This is an adaptation of the children's playground game.

As a listening version you are Grandma. For a speaking version your pupil takes that role. Grandma stands at one end of the room facing the wall and asks the players to repeat certain words or phrases while they inch forward to try to reach Grandma without being caught moving. Grandma at any time can spin around to try to catch someone moving.

For example, Grandma says, "Do you like apples?" The players repeat the question or reply to it as you wish. Grandma says, "Do you like pears?" At any point Grandma can spin around and try to catch someone moving.

Grandma can also say, "Left. Do you like ice cream?" Here the class must turn to the left to repeat the phrase, or reply with "yes I do", so Grandma has more chance of catching someone moving. Other actions could be, to the right, behind you, look up, look down, touch your nose and say, etc.

Guess the Action

Category: Speaking - good for present continuous
Level: Beginner to Intermediate
Materials: Picture or word flashcards
Age: 4 to 12
Pace: Wake up

How to play

Place a selection of pictures in a hat such as actions like running, sports, professions, animals or anything that involves doing something or miming. Draw out the first picture, look at it without your pupil seeing. Now mime the thing on that card while your pupil has ten-fifteen seconds to guess what it is. If successful give yourselves a point. Now swap over and let your pupil pick a card and mime for you to guess.

This game lends itself well to practising the present continuous as your pupil may use "you are running" and so on when guessing.

Guess the Word

Category: Spelling and speaking
Level: Beginner to Advanced
Materials: Pen and paper or the board
Age: 6 to Adult
Pace: Calm

Using words that your pupil knows start to spell out a word very slowly. For example say "it's an animal" and write the letter A. Wait a few seconds while your pupils tries to think of an animal starting with A. After five seconds you write the second letter in the word and continue until your pupil has guessed the word.

If your pupil guesses the word when you have only written the first letter award 100 points. If he or she guesses at the second letter award 50 points and continue to reduce the points scheme.

Then you have a turn. If your pupil needs help with spelling give him or her a hat with words written out. The child picks one and does not let you see it. Then play as above. You may also win points but to even the game up you may only win 30 points if you guess on the first letter, 20 points on the second and so on. Make up your own points scheme and if you find you are still winning easily adjust it so it becomes a close game with your pupil winning most of the time nonetheless - as this really encourages them.

GAMES H TO J

Category: Spelling and Speaking
Level: Beginner to Intermediate
Materials: Pen and paper
Age: 6 to 12
Pace: Calm

The hangman is drawn in eleven strokes like this:

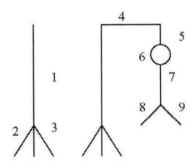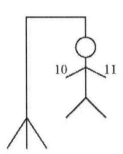

This is the classic hangman game of old. You decide on a word and write up the number of letters in that word with dashes. E.g. if the word were Dinosaur you would write up _ _ _ _ _ _ _ _. Your pupil has to guess what the word is by naming the letters of the alphabet. If the person guessing names a letter which is in the word, for example in this case the letter N, then you fill it into the blank: _ _ n _ _ _ _ _. If however a letter is named which is not part of the word, such as the letter E in this case, then you start to draw the "hangman". The drawing represents a man being hung from a noose. The idea is that the word must be guessed before the man is hung.

A useful variant when you want to work with only a few words is to have the pupil guess and spell all the words before a hangman is drawn. In this case you don't start a new hangman for every word but keep the same one for all the words. First let the pupil do the hangman and write the letters in. Then you swap. For example you are working with six words: jacket, hat, gloves, bag, sunglasses and keys. Your pupil has these word cards for reference and chooses one of them for you to guess first. The student writes out the dashes for the number of letters: _ _ _ _. Well it's totally obvious to you that the word is "keys" as it is the only word in the selection that has four letters, so you spell it out and the pupil writes in the letters. In fact this game works much better if the words are of the same length - such as "hat" and "bag".

A way round the fact that it's too easy for you to guess the word immediately by the number of letters is as follows: your pupil chooses one of the words and writes out the dashes but behind a screen, such as a book or box, so you do not know how many letters the word has. You then suggest letters and if these are not in the word your hangman is gradually drawn. Once you have guessed the first word continue on in the same way. Continue until you have guessed all the words. Then swap over.

Whichever way you play it it's a useful game to introduce the spelling of new words.

If you would prefer something less murderous than a hangman then make up your own little sketch - such as a cowboy's face, the nose being the last thing to go on. Here is an example of a non-violent alternative - a train. The last thing to be drawn is the smoke, which means that you have missed the train if you have not guessed the word by then. Draw this in eleven strokes also, first the round face, left eye, right eye, mouth, the whole body as the fifth stroke, each wheel one after the other, the chimney as the tenth stroke, and finally the smoke.

Hangman Additional Variant

Category: Speaking
Level: Beginner to Intermediate
Materials: Pen and paper or the board
Age: 6 to 12
Pace: Calm

Using the same drawings as above use Hangman to do more than letters and spelling. Here is an example using clothing words: You have a picture of a person in various clothes. Your pupil has to guess what the person is wearing before you finish the hangman.

First tell them if it is a man or a woman. If it is a man your group members can ask questions like "Is he wearing a shirt?" If he is wearing a shirt you draw it. If he is not wearing a shirt you start the hangman. This could also be a general guessing game using multiple question forms where pupils guess what is on a given picture. The object or activity depicted must be guessed before the hangman is completed.

Happy Families

Category: Speaking
Group size: 2 pupils plus parent/teacher minimum - cannot be played with two people
Level: Beginner to Lower Intermediate
Materials: Happy Families set (see bonus material)
Age: 4 to 12
Pace: Calm

Materials

For this game you need a set of Happy Families cards. You might find these on sale very cheaply in toy stores, and of course they are also easy to make. Your pupil could do this as a homework task.

How to Play

Shuffle and deal out one set of families. If you are a group of three with children over six then deal out six families. Younger pupils will not be able to handle holding so many cards so stick to one family each for them. The players have to take care not to show their cards to the others, and 4 to 6 year old children can't generally do this but it doesn't matter! In turn each player asks any other player for a member of one of the families. If the player asked has the family member he or she must hand it over. If he or she does not have it that is the end of the turn, and the next player in the circle asks for a family member. The idea is to be the first to collect a whole family.

Language Ideas

Players may use different questions. With beginners stick to one structure and insist on accuracy for this language drill.
Have you got Mr Smith? / Mrs, Miss, Master
Have you got daddy Smith? / mummy, brother, sister Have you got father Alien? / mother, son, daughter
Do you have?
I would like?
Please give me?
Can I have?
Please could I have?
Before you play Happy Families your players need to recognise and know the vocabulary for all of the family members involved, and also know the language you wish to revise. Play some of the other games such as Jump the Line, Rapid reaction, or Find the pairs memory game with the Happy Family cards first to familiarise everyone with the characters in the families.

Head to Head

Category: Listening (body parts)
Level: Beginner
Materials: A teddy or doll
Age: 3 to 7
Pace: Calm

Your pupil dances around to music until you stop it unexpectedly and issue a command such as "head to head". At this point your pupil must take his or her teddy bear (or doll) and touch heads with teddy.

Other ideas for commands are; hand to knee, nose to nose, eye to eye, cheek to cheek, foot to foot, mouth to ear, head to toe, hand in hand, back to back, ear to ear, hand to ear, back to front, foot to bottom, heel to toe, shoulder to shoulder, finger to finger, finger to nose etc.

Use this to teach body parts and revise them. When body parts are well known use it for possessives such as "touch teddy's head with your elbow" or "Peter's foot to mummy's/teacher's nose" and so on.

With siblings the two can play together and you may also add in toys as well to give more options.

Hidden Picture

Category: Speaking
Level: Beginner to Intermediate
Materials: Pictures and card with holes or slits cut into it
Age: 6 to 12
Pace: Calm to Wake up

Materials

Take a piece of A4 card and cut some small holes or slits into it. The easy versions have large holes and the harder ones have smaller holes. Using thick coloured paper is also an option, just check first that the paper or card is not see-through.

How to Play

Place the "hidden picture" card over a picture so that only parts of the picture show through the slits or holes. The players have to guess what the picture is behind the card. For children aged four you will want to use the easy hidden picture cards with bigger holes in them.

Hide and Guess

Category: Speaking
Level: Beginner to Lower Intermediate
Materials: Pictures or objects
Age: 3 to 12
Pace: Excitable

In this game one child hides behind something with a selection of flashcards or objects of the vocabulary. The child could hide behind a blanket hung up over two chairs, or behind a large piece of cardboard, or behind a piece of furniture.

On the floor behind the barrier are the picture cards you are working with. The child picks one out, or stands on it, or puts it in a hat, or selects it in some way or another. You now guess which card he or she has selected. When you guess the correct picture the child comes out from behind the barrier and shows you the card. Then you swap over.

For the most simple language the person guessing simply calls out the various words or asks a simple question like: Is it the train? Do you have the train? Have you got the train? Did you pick the train? Or use statements such as: It is the train. I think it is the train. You have the train. You picked the train.

The child behind the barrier replies with a suitable reply to the question such as: No it is not, no I haven't, or just plain no for the simplest answer.

If you are teaching beginners to lower intermediate levels then pick just one question and one answer and work with that until the child is using it fluently.

What will happen with the younger ones is that they will swap over cards behind the barrier because they will not want you to guess it right away, so to prevent that you may place the cards in a box, let the child pick one out without you seeing and go and hide behind the barrier with just that one card. Then you start to guess which one it is.

Hide and Seek Prepositions

Category: Speaking
Level: Beginner to Intermediate
Materials: Pebbles or other small items
Age: 3 to 12
Pace: Excitable

Hide pebbles or similar items all around the room. Play a song and for the duration of the song players search out the pebbles, trying to find as many as possible and making a note of where they find them. When the song ends the players describe where the pebbles or items are, for example: There's one under that book. There's one by the door.

With young children make the pebbles partially visible and in very easy places.

Higher or Lower

Category: Speaking
Level: Beginner
Materials: One or more packs of playing cards
Age: 3 to 12
Pace: Calm

Play this in pairs, either you and your pupil, or two pupils together. Each pair has a pack of playing cards or number cards. Each player states whether they think the next card will be higher or lower, if correct the player keeps the card and the idea is to collect as many cards as possible. Where there is a tie, i.e. if both players say "higher", then the card remains in the pile. The next time one of the pair wins they take the whole pile of unclaimed cards. Do numbers by having a player name the card that is turned over each time.

Language Ideas

Numbers and comparatives
For the higher numbers say that each number is x10 or x100 its face value. So 6 would become 60 or 600.

This is also an ideal game for comparatives such as "5 is higher than 4", "3 is lower than 10", etc. Use this game also to drill "more than" and "less than", and "the same as".

A variant on this game is to use sets of picture cards. Here is an example with animals: Each time a card is turned over the players guess whether the next one will be bigger or smaller, (in real life, not in the picture). Other examples that spring to mind are people, who can be taller, shorter, thinner, fatter, more cautious than or prettier, etc. Additionally use pictures of types of transport, which can be faster or slower. If you do not have any pictures use word flash cards instead.

Hoops or circles

Category: Listening
Level: Beginner
Materials: pictures and hoops or circles on the floor
Age: 3 to 10
Pace: Wake up

Place hoops or circles in the corners and around the room or teaching area. Each hoop has either a picture or a colour in it. The child skips round the room and when you call out the colour or picture they must jump into the right hoop.

If you have these hoops they may be used for all sorts of other games, such as having the children jump through them and name the picture the other side, or rolling the hoops along the floor. However if you do not have any hoops but you do have an old sheet or some old material, then cut this material into circles, and the children jump onto those, but only with a carpet floor, as material on tiles or wood will slip.

Hop Bunny Hop

Category: Listening
Level: Beginner
Materials: None
Age: 3 to 10
Pace: Wake up

This is a lovely game for three year old children. Ask your pupil to hop around like bunnies until you shout out, Danger - a fox! The child must freeze. If he or she moves he is out and you swap over. You then say, It's OK, the danger's gone. The child hops about again until you call out the next thing. Some children will cry and feel they have failed if you catch them moving so in that case it is best to pretend not to notice.

This game is good for animals, but you could make something up for any language. For example let us imagine that you want to teach food. You could have a scenario where there are these giant portions of food as big as a house and if you are caught moving when you should be freezing you would have to eat the whole thing. Then you would say, Danger, or Watch out, a giant burger!

Vary this idea by playing music and telling the children to hop round like bunnies while the music plays. When the music stops they must freeze. Then you tell them what the next animal will be and they pretend to be that animal when the music starts again.

Other vocabulary you could use for this idea are actions, or make believe such as pretend you are a doctor, or pretend you are eating an ice cream, etc.

Hot Potato

Category: Speaking
Group size: 2 or more - teacher or parent needs minimum of 2 pupils
Level: Beginner to Intermediate
Materials: A potato or any object.
Age: 4 to 12
Pace: Wake up

Have your pupils face each other, and close your eyes. The players pass the potato to each other as quickly as they can, and must take it when it comes to them, until you shout out "Hot Potato!" and open your eyes to see who has the potato. The player holding it has to answer a question, or do a forfeit, such as pretending to be a giraffe, or doing a forward roll.

To introduce more vocabulary than just "Hot Potato" have the players say a rhyme or sing while they pass the potato back and forth.

An easy variant is to pass a word or picture flash card, which each player calls out in turn. This is good when at the early stage of learning new vocabulary. Give them a new card every round so they say a different word.

For a more advanced version as the potato is passed back and forth, each player must say a word beginning with a certain letter, so if the letter was B, players could say any word beginning with B. A word cannot be used twice. If they cannot think of a word they must hold the potato while they keep thinking – increasing their chance of being caught with it.

A variant of this is to say any word as long as it is part of a given theme such as an animal, or a profession, or a type of building such as bank, supermarket, etc., or a country, or a colour. After each round change the theme or the letter.

Another more advanced variant is that the player must think of a word that begins with the last letter of the previous word. If player one says "bat", player two can say any word beginning with "T", such as "tripod", player three must now think of any word beginning with the letter "D" and so on.

I spy

Category: Speaking
Level: Beginner to Intermediate
Materials: Pictures on the walls or floor are useful
Age: 4 to 10
Pace: Calm

This is the classic game that so many of us have played on a long car journey during which we drove the adults spare asking if we were nearly there yet, barely had we left the house. One player looks around the room, or garden and secretly chooses an item. You could have them draw the item to prevent them changing their minds mid-game, which does have a tendency of happening!

The player then says "I spy with my little eye, something beginning with ___" (whichever letter of the alphabet the item they have decided on begins with). For example if they have decided on a "blue bag" they will say, "I spy with my little eye something beginning with B". The other players then have to guess the item by calling out possibilities such as "book" or "bicycle".

Joker

Category: Speaking - question and answer game
Level: Beginner to Intermediate
Materials: Pack of playing cards
Age: 4 to 12
Pace: Calm

The aim of the game is to get rid of all your cards by answering questions correctly or naming vocabulary items.

Deal out half a pack of playing cards including the jokers between you and your pupil/s. The players must not look at their cards but place them face down on the table or floor.

Prepare questions beforehand on pieces of paper, or use vocabulary flashcards, or place objects in a bag.

Turn over the first question or picture card, or have your pupil reach into the mystery bag and pull out an item. Your pupil now names that word or answers the question on the paper. Use questions your pupil knows, not brand new ones. Revise familiar things such as "what's your name?", "what colour is a banana?" and so on. If your pupil is more advanced then adjust the level of questions to suit.

Your pupil answers and turns over a playing card from his or her pile. If this card is any card except a joker, then it is taken out of the game, provided the pupil answered the question correctly. If the answer is incorrect that card is placed in a pile in the centre.

When your pupil turns up the joker he or she must collect all the discarded cards from the pile in the middle, UNLESS he or she has answered the question correctly, in which case the joker is taken out of the game and the teacher or parent has to pick up all the cards in the centre. You may like to add in extra jokers from other packs to increase interest. Now it's the parent or teacher's turn. Select a question, answer it, turn up one of your cards. If the card is a joker the teacher or parent has to collect all the cards in the middle. If it is any other card then the teacher can take that card out of the game.

Hopefully the pupil will have a fair chance against the teacher or parent because the teacher has to pick up all the cards in the centre when a joker appears. It's best if you help your pupil answer the question correctly so that YOU collect the cards in the centre - unless you are MILES behind and you want the game to be closer.

You may complicate the game for variety with older children by saying for example that any child turning up an ace may keep it as a "life-saver" against a potential future joker.

Language ideas

Use any question forms you like. Use the same question form over and over for a simple level and mix up various types of questions for revision games or for more advanced levels.

Jump the Line

Category: Listening
Level: Beginner to Intermediate
Materials: Picture or word flashcards and/or the board
Age: 4 to 12
Pace: Wake up

This game is ideal during the initial presentation stage of new vocabulary. Designate an imaginary line or make one with string or tape and place pictures or words either side of that line, to the left and to the right. If you teach in a classroom with no space at all draw a vertical line down the middle of the board and stick up or draw pictures or words either side of the line. Now call out the items and the players must jump to the right or to the left depending on the location of the picture in relation to the line.

Language ideas

Use this game to present new vocabulary, and also to familiarise players with a grammatical structure by repeating the same sentence each time, with a different noun represented by the picture or word on the board. Call out actress, singer, businessman, if you are learning the professions for the first time. Call out a sentence such as, "I'd like to be an actress" or, "I'd like to be a singer" to revise professions and introduce the conditional. Do not introduce new vocabulary and a new structure in the same game.

GAMES K TO M

Keep a Straight Face

Category: Listening game or Revision for Question forms
Level: Beginner to Intermediate
Materials: None or prepare questions ahead of time
Age: 4 to 12
Pace: Wake up

Your pupil thinks up questions to ask you. Your pupil asks you the first question to which you reply correctly. From now on all questions must be answered with this same reply without anyone laughing or smiling. So the first question might be: Where do you live? The reply will be something like: Hong Kong. The next question might be: What's your name? Or What do you feed your pet? The reply must be: Hong Kong. If either teacher or pupil smile or has any expression other than a dead-pan straight face then he or she is loses a point.

Use this as a listening game with you asking the questions to let your pupil hear question forms repeatedly. When using it as a speaking game it works best as a revision game for question forms, or with a pre-prepared list of questions.

Laughing Game

Category: Silly game - speaking
Level: Beginner to Intermediate
Materials: A feather, tissue or light object
Age: 4 to 12
Pace: Wake up

This is a silly game to lighten up. Throw something light such as a feather, a tissue or a scarf into the air and you both laugh and giggle and roll around in feigned hysterics until the object touches the floor, at which point you freeze and be silent. Anyone who giggles has to do a forfeit, such as naming a flashcard or doing something silly. This game can take a few goes to get into, so don't be put off by the idea of having to act - it will happen naturally. First just do your best pretending to laugh, even if it sounds totally fake. As you play a few times the interaction between the two of you will make you laugh naturally.

Listen

Category: Listening
Level: Beginner to Intermediate
Materials: A long scarf is useful but not obligatory
Age: 4 to 12
Pace: Wake up

This game is excellent for practising new vocabulary or for revising.

Stand in a space with your pupil either touching you with an outstretched hand, or holding onto the end of a scarf. Although this kind of prop is optional, the children love it.

You repeat vocabulary or sentences that you are teaching while your pupil must stay touching you or holding the scarf until you say a magic word. When you say that word the child runs to touch the wall and you try to catch him or her. It is generally best never to catch young children as it can make them sad and feel as though they failed, so be sensitive to this, and make a convincing attempt to catch them, but just miss!

So for example start by naming the magic word, it could be "mother". You now start to say words such as father, brother, sister, grandmother etc. When you say, mother, the child must run off and you try and touch him or her before he or she reaches the safe zone. If you do not want to run then just try and touch the child before he or she has let go of you, or the scarf, without you actually moving from the spot. If you only have a small space make a rule where you are allowed to take one step only.

Great variety can be added to this game by changing the way you say the words. Sometimes use a flat monotone for several words and then suddenly say a word with great enthusiasm. This alone can make some children let go of you even though you did not say the magic word.

You may also add variety by changing the set up. For example you may have the child seated near you on the floor. When you say the magic word the pupil must get up and move away to safety. Also use ideas such as having the child balance on one leg while listening out for the magic word and then clap and run away on hearing it. If a child cannot balance, or forgets to clap before running away he or she does a forfeit.

Your pupil may want a turn chasing you too!

Language ideas to use with this game

This game lends itself to any vocabulary. You may also use short sentences by way of revision, or in preparation for introducing those phrases properly later in the lesson, or in the next lesson. For example you could have the word "train" as the magic word and say, I like buses, I like cars, I like planes, I like trains! Replace the phrase I like with anything. For example if you want to teach the past continuous then the magic word can be "reading" and you say sentences such as I was driving, I was walking, I was reading!

In the video demo we used animals and the magic words were "I'm hungry!" On hearing those words Anna had to let go of the scarf and run to the tree.

Make A Sentence (or a Question)

Category: Speaking and Writing variant
Level: Beginner to Intermediate
Materials: None. Bells or buzzers optional
Age: 6 to Adult
Pace: Calm

How to Play

Spell a word out loud. Your pupil says the word for one point, and then says a sentence with the word in it for three points. To add spice, have a time limit for these two tasks of 10-15 seconds.

Use this with general English or be specific about what you practise. To focus in on a specific structure specify that the sentence must be in a certain tense, or using a certain phrase.

This game is adaptable to any language at all. Here is a simple version: Spell out different foods and the children make up sentences or questions about whether they like or dislike them.

A variant is to hold up a picture or word and say 'sentence' or 'question'. Your pupil must come up with something. Take it in turns if you have two pupils. For example, you hold up a picture of, or say the word "ice-cream" and then say "question", the students must think of a question with that word in it such as; "Do you like ice-cream?" or "Can I have some ice-cream please?" or "Is there any ice-cream?"

Intermediate to advanced variant

A variant of this game is that with each word that you give out the players must come up with a sentence as part of a story which they make up as the game goes along. For a writing version for English composition spell out the word and let your pupil(s) produce a sentence with the word in it. If you have two pupils they can decide if each other's sentence is correct grammatically and if so award a point.

Making Up Stories

Category: Speaking and Writing
Level: Intermediate to Advanced
Materials: Random pictures
Age: 8 to 12
Pace: Calm

How to Play

Using a series of random pictures make up a story with your pupil. Your pupil picks out the first picture and starts the story with a sentence. You then continue the story, either by saying more about the first picture, or by picking a second picture and bringing that into the story. The story can be plausible or ridiculous as the mood takes you. The important thing is that the grammar and use of language is correct. This game is a fun challenge and uses the imagination, rather than following the often dull and obvious story lines of picture composition prompts usually provided in language books.

Language and Marking

Keep the English simple to stay within the bounds of your pupil's knowledge. You may want to give the tense the story takes place in - for example it was yesterday, it is happening now, or it is someone telling the story of what they plan to do in the future.

Matching and Mirroring

Category: Listening
Level: Beginner to Intermediate
Materials: None
Age: 3 to 9
Pace: Wake up

Matching and mirroring is known in the art of NLP (Neuro-Linguistic-Programming) for its capacity to bond people together. People often subconsciously mirror each other and this shows that there is some sort of bond or connection taking place. Consciously copying each other will also create a bond, between you and your pupil.

This game is particularly good for introducing body parts and actions. You name an action, such as "jump five times", you do it and your pupil copies you, not just jumping five times but jumping in the way that you jump! If you say "touch your nose" and you touch your own nose with your toe, then your pupil must do the same. Or if you touch your nose with your forefinger your pupil also uses his or her forefinger. If you stick your tongue out while doing it then your pupil does the same.

This game allows you to use quite a bit of English without worrying whether your pupil understands every single word as he or she will be watching your actions.

Increase the difficulty of the language according to the level from simple commands to more imaginative language and actions such as waving in the wind like a field of corn.

Match Up

Category: Speaking
Level: Lower intermediate to Advanced
Materials: Picture or word flashcards
Age: 4 to 12
Pace: Calm

Think up pairs of words that go together, such as hair and hairbrush and have either a picture of hair and another of a hairbrush, or two word flashcards with one word on each. Shuffle and deal out these cards between you and your pupil. You must not let each other see your cards.

With younger children (three to four), you need to give out identical pairs of pictures so they can match dog with dog, rather than dog with bone or basket.

The object of the game is to match up the pairs so players start by taking out any pairs that they hold and laying them down face up. In order to get the points for those pairs the player has to name the items or make a sentence up with the words in.

Now let your pupil start by asking you a question in order to win a card from you. Let's say your pupil is holding a picture of an apple and the matching card is either another apple or another fruit. Your pupil asks: "Do you like apples?" You then reply with "Yes I do." and hand over the apple picture. Your pupil now has a pair to lay down. Continue until all pairs are made.

With four to six year old children play as above. With older children have one card that does not have a pair. The player left with that card at the end loses.

More language Ideas

Use this game any language. For example if you want to do professions, she's a, he's a, and places of work give out one set of cards of people doing jobs and another set of the places they work. For example:
Doctor and hospital
Nurse and doctor's surgery
Singer and club
Actor and stage
Footballer and football pitch
Shop assistant and shop

Hairdresser and hairdressers. Etc.

Advanced Version

For the advanced version players must guess whether the other item matches theirs by asking questions about it and they are not allowed to name the item. Miming is not allowed. If they have a brush however they can ask something specific such as, "Is your item anything to do with hair?" This version requires a huge amount of language and you might want to discuss some ideas of questions before getting started.

For example:
Is it part of a human body?
Is it something an animal has?
Is it something an animal/human would use?
Is it large or small?
Would a person use it in the morning?
Would a person use it to clean their teeth?
Is it edible / something we would eat?
Can you _____ with it?

Memory Game

Category: Speaking
Level: Beginner to Intermediate
Materials: Picture or word flashcards
Age: 4 to 12
Pace: Calm

This is a classic list making game where vocabulary can be repeated many times. It is excellent for reinforcing and revising words. The first player says a word, player B says the first word and adds one. Back to the first player who repeats the first two words and adds one, and so on.

Use any scenario for this game such as: I went shopping and I bought an apple. I went shopping and I bought an apple and a banana. I went shopping and I bought an apple, a banana and a pear. etc. If necessary display picture flashcards to help the younger children remember.

Language ideas
This game is adaptable to a multitude of language uses, for example:

There is/there are: In my wardrobe there are socks, there are shoes, there is a dress, there are shirts, there is a scarf etc.

Her name is/His name is: Her name is Barbie, his name is Ken, her name is Rita, and his name is Paul etc.

She's a/he's a: She's a model, he's an action man, she's a nurse, he's a doctor, etc.

She likes/she does not like

Playing sports: He plays golf, he plays tennis, he goes riding, he windsurfs, etc.

Past tense: Yesterday for supper I had milk, chocolate, pizza, etc.

Memory Game With Sound Effects

A fun way to play the above game is with sound effects. This would be a listening game. The first player does the sound effects for a train, the second must do a train and another method of transport. Do this with animals, or with emotions such as be happy, be sad, laugh, cry, sing, shout, whisper. The parent or teacher names the item to mime such as "happy" and you both take turns to act it. The teacher then provides a second thing to act, or the pupil can do this if he or she has the vocabulary. You then act out "happy" followed by the second action and so on, until you have difficulty remembering the order of things. Don't worry if you are both a bit serious to start out with - you will both start laughing naturally as the game loosens you both up.

Easy, intermediate and advanced variations

For advanced players have them make up and memorize a story. You could give them a specific tense that you would like them to work on. Use picture cards for them to weave into the story or not as you like. As the phrases created will be repeated over and over it is worth ensuring they are correct in order to avoid inadvertently reinforcing errors, for that reason this is best as a structured speaking exercise to reinforce a particular grammatical feature rather than a free-speaking exercise. Ask players to write the story up from memory afterwards if you wish.

Another way to play that is more intermediate is to give each child a line of the story. The first player reads out the first line of the story. The second player must memorise it, repeat it and add their line. The third player repeats the first two lines and adds his or line and so on. Keep the sentences short so that they are easy to remember.

Miming Games

Category: Listening or speaking
Level: Beginner to Lower Intermediate
Materials: None
Age: 3 to 12
Pace: Calm

Young children LOVE to mime and they love doing actions. Use miming to work on vocabulary or sentences which you would like them to hear repeatedly, either as part of initial presentation of the language, or as revision.

If you are presenting new language tell the children what to mime in English and demonstrate yourself, or show a picture. The children copy you. Switch to a new word, repeating the word and miming while they copy. Keep this up introducing four new words at a time. Gradually stop miming so the children have to rely on understanding, and you just tell them what to mime.

For speaking skills mime something and your pupil guesses what you are doing. Your student may also suggest things for to mime. To help with this lay out some cards face down. Player A takes a card and looks at it without player B seeing. He or she then mimes what is on the card and player B has to guess what is being mimed.

Miming games can be adapted to a wide range of vocabulary. Here are some examples:

Mime eating different foods - ice cream, pasta, chewy toffees, chewing gum, hot dog, chips, steak, etc.

Mime a member of the family - mum, dad, baby, sister, brother, grandfather, great-grandmother, etc.

Mime an action - close the curtains, knock on the door, sit on the floor, stand up, see, look, run, walk, sleep, cry, sing, dance, play tennis, play football

Mime a feeling - happy, sad, angry, sleepy, dreamy, tired

Mime an animal - mime the animal with or without sound effects

Mime a job - doctor, nurse, taxi driver, schoolteacher, footballer, racing driver, farmer, opera singer, actor, clown, circus acrobat, etc.

Mime a type of transport with sound effects

Use an unlimited number of make believe type mimes along the lines of the things your children like doing. Examples are:

Driving a car at 100 miles per hour (160 km),

Pretending to be a fairy, a princess, a witch, a pirate, a cowboy, a prince, a knight, a warrior, a character from Star Wars or a cartoon they know, a dancer, a rock star, singer, a clown, a lion tamer, doctors and patients, which is good for listening for body parts

You may also have the children mime any subject that is related to the vocabulary or language you want to teach. For example:

Show us how you would chase a dog.

Show us how you would pick a beautiful flower.

Show us how you would hop like a rabbit.

Show us how you would eat a cake.

Musical Vocabulary

Category: Listening
Level: Beginner
Materials: Sets of picture cards
Age: 3 to 7
Pace: Wake up to Excitable

How to Play

Spread picture cards on the floor and have your pupil dance or jump in a circle around the pictures while you play music. Stop the music unpredictably and call out one of the picture cards, or a sentence containing one of the picture cards, such as "hamburger" or "I'd like a hamburger". The player jumps on the relevant picture.

This game appeals greatly to girls as they often love dancing and prancing about - let them choose the music to use with the game or play something you know they like. Probably you will be able to use this with girls up to age 7 or older whereas with boys use it until and including age 5.

If you do not have music the players can circle round the pictures chanting a rhyme or singing and at the end of each verse or song the picture card is called out.

Mystery Bag

Category: Speaking and Spelling Option
Level: Beginner
Materials: A non see-through cloth bag or bag and a selection of items

Age: 4 to 12
Pace: Calm

Give each of your pupils a black bag containing a few mystery items. Your pupil feels the items in the bag and tells you what they are.

You, or the players write up the items. If you have two pupils do not look in the bags yet, but swap them over. Let the pupils guess and write down the items in their new bag and then reveal the contents and compare.

Speaking opportunities are things like "It's an apple", "I think it's an apple", "There is an apple in the bag".

Use any objects that you have to hand and here are some examples to give you ideas: pens, a rubber, a calculator, an old pair of glasses, a roll of tape, a CD Rom, a spoon, toys such as Barbie, mini cars, an apple, an orange, a tennis ball, a ping pong ball, a plastic mug, a piece of paper, medium-sized plastic animals and dinosaurs if you have them, their favourite toys such as Spiderman, or whatever is 'in' at the time, etc.

Tip: Younger children can feel the items by placing one of their hands inside the bag while the teens or adults can try to guess by only feeling the outside of the bag – which is much harder.

GAMES N TO P

Name and Chase

Category: Speaking
Level: Beginners to Lower Intermediate
Materials: Pictures
Age: 4 to 12
Pace: Wake up to Excitable

This game can be used for revising vocabulary you have covered during the term or in previous terms or years. You may also use it for any kind of question and answer format.

Place a pile of picture cards of known vocabulary cards face down between you and your pupil. Your pupil turns the top card over and names the vocabulary or makes a question or sentence using the word. For example if the first card is a banana the drill might be to ask, "Where is the banana?" The next card is an apple so the pupil says, "Where is the apple?" and so on. Use whatever grammar/sentence structure you wish to focus on for the game. An advanced game would be for the pupil to make up a sentence from scratch using the word banana. Continue through the pack of cards like this. You may alternate with your pupil turning the cards over and giving the answers.

Now for the fun part of this game. Hidden within the pack of pictures are some blank cards, which will be the "chase" cards. These must be the same size and shape as the others so no one knows when a blank card is coming. Alternatively decide beforehand which cards will be "chase" cards, for example the pizza pictures. Whoever turns over a "chase" card has to get up and run to a wall in the room before the other player has time to touch him or her.

Modify where you run and what you have to touch to be safe according to your teaching space. Make it easy for your pupil and hard for you. If the pupil is older, make it equally hard for both of you. If the person turning over the "chase" card makes it to the safe spot without being touched the game continues. If the person does not make it and is caught by the other player then the player caught does a forfeit such as pretending to be a chicken. See the forfeit list for ideas.

Noughts And Crosses

Category: Speaking / Reading
Level: Beginners to Lower Intermediate
Materials: Noughts and Crosses sets - see below
Age: 4 to 12
Pace: Calm

You probably already know this game. It is also known as Tic Tac Toe in America. Noughts and crosses is a paper and pencil game where each player tries to make a row of three. A grid consists of nine spaces in three rows of three. A row of three can be horizontal, vertical or diagonal.

Player one places a cross in one of the boxes. Player two now selects an empty box to play a nought or zero. Player one writes in a second cross, player two a second nought and so on until someone achieves a row of three or there are no more spaces to play in.

For the language version of this place nine vocabulary pictures or words in a grid of three rows of three. Instead of writing in a cross or a zero players will instead place an item on a picture card and try to make a row of three items. Player one could use pen lids while player two uses paper clips for example. Player one attempts to make a row of three pen lids while blocking player two from making a row of three paper clips.

To place a pen lid or paper clip the player must name the vocabulary in the picture - or alternatively use the word in a sentence. As usual sentences may be structured for specific grammar or for more advanced pupils use any kind of language.

Reading Variant

Play noughts and crosses using word flash cards to introduce the way words are written before moving on to writing and spelling games. Each player has five word flashcards with the same word, so the teacher may have five cards with "jacket" written on them while the pupil has five cards with "hat". Using an imaginary grid take it in turns to place your cards and try to make a row of three.

Oranges

Category: Speaking
Level: Beginners to Lower Intermediate
Materials: Oranges or round objects such as balls or potatoes
Age: 6 to 12. Teens may enjoy this too depending on the individuals.
Pace: Wake up

Place three oranges per person on a piece of furniture. Underneath each orange is a word flashcard. At other points in the room or house, are pictures representing the words. Each player picks up an orange under his or her chin - no hands allowed - and walks to the pictures with the orange held under the chin. On arriving at the pictures the player gets down on the ground/close to the picture and carefully places the orange on the correct picture.

So you could have three pictures in a group on the floor for each player. Players travel from the oranges to the pictures and place each orange on a picture in turn - matching the word with the picture. Or you might want to spread the pictures about the room so that players have to walk about searching for the matching picture, all the while holding the orange under the chin with no hands.

The whole thing is a race between the players from start to placing the last orange. Oranges MUST be on the picture and not to the side or near it. If a player drops an orange while in transit he or she has to get down on the ground and pick it up again with the chin and neck without touching it. If you see your competitor struggling then you always have the option of "accidentally" dropping your orange. You might also allow younger pupils to use their hands three times. If playing with children aged nine or older then the competition will be fierce! And no cheating! With a bit of luck they will be better at it than you and win even though you are trying your hardest.

Phonemes - Some Thoughts on Teaching the Phonemic Alphabet

If you are not familiar with phonemes and don't want to teach that way you might still want to use these suggested games below but with pictures or words.

Learning phonemes individually is not essential in order to speak a language well. This is a fact as I learned several languages fluently with no conscious knowledge of individual phonemes. However I hasten to add that the languages I learned were all related to English with the same Indo-European and then Anglo-Saxon or Latin roots.

Practice with phonemes can help enormously when learning a non-related language such as a Thai person learning English. Phonemes would be less essential with a German person learning English where many sounds are the same and there are relatively few totally new sounds. As well as making things easier for the student once the new phonemes are learned, this knowledge gives independence from the teacher in working out pronunciation.

Many teachers shy away from teaching phonemes so how can you decide if you need to teach them? I would say quite simply listen to the results you are achieving in your lessons. If you clearly hear that you have some pronunciation issues that lead to confusion in meaning then it is worth taking a step back to learn phonemes. I say take a step back because it can feel like that. However with this solid foundation in pronunciation your students may become better English speakers in the medium to long term.

Do not expect to see amazing results right away. You need to work with phonemes regularly, little and often. New neural pathways need to be built as students learn the facial and tongue position for each new sound, some of which will be utterly new to them and their muscles will need to integrate these new shapes and sounds.

Use any of the games in this book to teach phonemes and phonemic script - just as if you were teaching a new vocabulary word, teach a sound instead, with or without the symbol.

Phoneme Hangman

Category: Saying sounds
Level: Beginner to Intermediate
Materials: None
Age: 6 to Adult
Pace: Calm

Use this game if you are teaching phonemes with phonemic script. This game allows students to say sounds and see what they look like in phonemic script. It helps young learners understand that phonemic script is made up of sounds and not letters. They also see an instant transcription of the sounds they make into the script.

Think of a word and the phonemic script for it such as the word wish. Write out __ __ __. The pupil guesses which sounds are in the word by making a sound, which you then transcribe as phonemic script. If the sound is in the word you fill in one of the blanks. If not you write that symbol on the board so students can see what it looks like. If students give you sounds that are already on the board point to the corresponding symbol. Students continue until the word is filled in.

Phoneme Match

Category: Recognising new phonemes and revising them

Level: All levels to learn phonemes and improve pronunciation
Materials: Words on cards
Age: 6 to 12
Pace: Wake up

Put 2 to 4 phoneme symbols on the table. If you are revising you may use a greater number. Use fewer with younger children. If you see children are struggling then play with fewer symbols. Write out about five words for each sound on cards or paper and shuffle them. Take it in turns to pick a word card from the pile, pronouncing the word and match it to the correct phoneme. For listening skills when introducing the phonemes you say the sound and the pupil matches it to the correct phoneme. For speaking the pupil says the sound. If correct the pupil keeps that word card, the aim being to collect as many as possible during the game. If incorrect the card is out of the game. Play a second round with the same words and see if the pupil wins more word cards in round two.

Phonemes - Wall Charts

Category: Recognising phonemes
Level: All levels to learn phonemes and improve pronunciation
Materials: Large pieces of coloured paper, or plain paper and coloured

pens

Age: 6 to 12
Pace: Wake up

This is an ongoing activity that can be done over a term while introducing and learning phonemes. For each phoneme use a matching picture such as a picture of cheese for the long /i:/ sound. After some initial drilling using a simple listening game like Jump the Line, which you play with 2 or more phonemes, stick up a large piece of paper on the wall with the phoneme and the picture at the top and the word 'cheese' written underneath. In the first lesson you may only have two of these pieces of paper on the wall and you will add to them over the coming lessons until you have all the 42 phonemes up, or all the most relevant phonemes for your English language learners.

Next play Show Me where you call out a phoneme and the child points to the correct wall chart. In the same lesson and in subsequent lessons give out words on cards and give the student a time limit to stick their word or words on the correct chart. Use pictures or words for this. For example a child with a picture of some feet will stick the picture or word card on the "cheese" wall chart.

As a variation give your pupil a pile of words and explain that all the words must be stuck to the correct wall chart before the end of the song. Play a short song and say "Go". If you see your pupil is not going to make it on time give some help. Err on the side of always making it easy enough for the pupil to complete. As the pupil improves he or she gets more cards to stick up in the same amount of time.

Pictionary

Category: Speaking
Level: Beginners to Intermediate
Materials: Paper and pens
Age: 5 to 12
Pace: Wake up

This is the classic Pictionary game where one player draws an object and the other player tries to be the first to guess what it is. This game works well with one person drawing and two guessing but it's also fine in pairs.

Each person takes a turn to draw an object which the other must guess. Take it in turns to pick a picture from a pile and draw it.

Picture Flashcards

Category: Speaking
Level: Beginners to Advanced
Materials: Picture flash cards
Age: 4 to 12
Pace: Calm

For lightening speed vocabulary revision hold up pictures and have your player call out the name of the item. Allow a few seconds per picture, decreasing to one second per picture as your pupil improves. Those correctly named are earned as points. Any not known are left aside. At the end of the round play a listening game on the words that were not known.

To make the game exciting show each picture for a maximum of 2 seconds and go through the flashcards quicker if the children can keep up.

If you are working with two pupils try this collaboration: The two pupils must win as many cards as possible between them. Taking it in turns to name a card each pupil adds any card successfully name to a communal pile. At the end shuffle the cards that were not known and go through them once again. Then count up how many words the pupils named between them. This avoids competition between siblings and friends, which can have disastrous consequences.

Ping Pong

Category: Reading, Writing and Speaking
Level: Beginners to Intermediate
Materials: Paper and pens
Age: 6 to adult
Pace: Calm

Give a time limit for pupils to write down as many words as possible in a given theme. When the time is up take it in turns to call out one word. You must hit back with a different word until one of you runs out of new words. The winner is the one that speaks last.

Needless to say make sure you say more obscure words and leave the easy ones for your pupil. For example if doing colours leave red, blue, yellow and green for your pupil while you use beige, indigo, ochre and scarlet. In addition,while your pupil is allowed to make a list of words in advance (good excuse for some writing and spelling practice), you are not allowed to prepare anything. Your pupil may prepare transport for example and then you pull your theme out of a hat, or think one up on the spur of the moment - so you have to think of words off the cuff. If you pupil has the transport theme and you have book titles the game would go like this: Pupil: "bus". Teacher: "The Lion, The Witch and the Wardrobe". Pupil: "train". Teacher: "Charlie and the Chocolate Factory". And so on.

As with most of the games, this one is very adaptable. It is up to you to make the language and vocabulary as hard or as easy as you like. Use categories of words such as sports or food, or play with short sentences like, "I'm French, I'm Spanish, I'm English" and so on.

Use simple vocabulary revision for this game, or have the pupils call out a sentence, which includes a word from the theme and your desired target structure. Drill the target structure with some step three speaking games beforehand so this game flows well.

Point and Spin

Category: Speaking
Level: Beginners to Intermediate
Materials: None
Age: 4 to 8
Pace: Wake up

How to Play

This is for the younger ones who will enjoy the novelty of the blindfold and spinning around. Place your child in the centre of a circle of picture flashcards wearing a blindfold. Spin the child around while you say a rhyme or play a few bars of music. When the rhyme stops your pupil points downwards in the direction of the flashcards and says a word - hoping to guess the word that is showing on the flashcard. If correct the pupil wins that card. Continue playing until the pupil has had ten goes. The aim is to correctly guess three cards before the ten goes are up.

Here is an example of how to play this game using vocabulary for professions: Spread out pictures of people doing professions on the floor in a circle, well spaced out. It's quite possible to make the game easier by having the same pictures several times. Show the pupil one of the pictures such as 'doctor' and then put the blindfold on. The child spins while you say the rhyme, which can be anything you like, such as:

What does he do? do be do do,
Do be do do, What does he do?
OR
What does he do? Buzz, buzz, buzz.
I want to know what he does!

The child spins round and when the rhyme stops points at a card saying, "He's a doctor", hoping that the card is in fact a doctor picture. Remove the blindfold and let the pupil look to see what the picture is.

Potato Race

Category: Speaking
Level: Beginners to Intermediate
Materials: Potatoes and spoons
Age: 4 to 12
Pace: Wake up to Excitable

This game is an excuse to ask and answer questions while racing with a potato balanced on a spoon. As children we played this game with boiled eggs. It's more fun as a team game but the little ones still really enjoy it.

How to Play

Have a start line and a line at the other end of the room, or in a different room. At the start line have four flashcards per person. At the other line have four potatoes each on the ground. In order to start each player must name one of the flashcards. When this language ritual has been completed the race is on. Both players run down the end of the room, pick up a potato with the spoon and race back to the start line, placing the potato on one of the flashcards.

The teacher has the handicap of not being able to touch the potato and has to get it on the spoon solely by using the spoon - and no body part –

whereas young children may be allowed to use their hands. With older children who are dexterous, this is not necessary and teacher and pupil can compete for real. With aged four you might want to reduce the distance they have to travel with their potatoes. It's possible to introduce penalties if a player drops their potato, such as starting at the beginning again, or having to say three words in English on the spot before continuing.

Language Ideas

Use the flashcards with any vocabulary. Alternatively make up a sentence or question and answer using the word on the card. The language ritual prior to running for the potatoes can be that the teacher asks the pupil a question such as "Where are you from?" The pupil has a series of country picture cards on the floor and answers, "I'm from Mexico" at which you both of you set off on the spoon race.

One can also do away with the flashcards totally and simply have a language exchange at the start line before running for the potatoes.

Prepositions

Category: Speaking
Level: Beginner
Materials: pack of playing cards
Age: 4 to adult
Pace: Wake up

Choose four preposition words such as, "between, in front of, behind, next to". Place some objects such as books on the table. Sit at one side of the table with your pupil and define where in space those positions are. So you might have two books next to each other. Between will be in between those two books. In front of will be the near side of the books, behind will be the far side of the books and next to can be the outer edge of one of the books.

Now match a playing card suit to each of these places. So hearts can be between, spades next to, clubs behind and diamonds in front of. The teacher has the pack of cards behind his or her back. Reach behind and pull out a card. As soon as you see the card you race to touch the correct location, saying the preposition simultaneously. So if the teacher pulls out a diamond you both race to touch the spot that means in front of, and so on.

At first it is quite slow as you both memorise which suit matches the correct spot. After a few goes the game naturally speeds up. It is important that the teacher pulls out the playing card so as to be at a disadvantage. As always let the younger ones beat you. With the older ones try your best - you may find they beat you hands down!

After you have played with four prepositions by all means make the game more complex by adding in more prepositions, such as on top of, underneath, opposite. Attribute a new colour and position to each new preposition. If using playing cards attribute any king to on top of, any queen to underneath and any jack to opposite.

In the video demo of this game with Julie we are using sticks with coloured bands on them rather than playing cards. Those sticks are from a game where you have to pick out a stick without any of the others moving but we used them for prepositions.

Preposition Obstacles

Category: Listening
Level: Beginner
Materials: pack of playing cards
Age: 4 to 10
Pace: Wake up

Lay out a few items to climb over or crawl under or through, such as a blanket or a chair. Any object can be stepped over. A hoop could be something they go through. You could even just use large pieces of cardboard. You each have a piece of card and you tell each other what to do with it, for example to go under it, or over it, to stand behind it, to sit on it, or similar. You may make this a race where the child carries out the action before you count to five and then runs to the wall for safety. After you have counted to five run and catch the child, but not if they are in the safe zone.

Pronunciation Chart Game

Category: Speaking - thinking about pronunciation
Level: Beginner to Advanced
Materials: Word cards
Age: 6 to adult
Pace: Calm

This is a version of the Phonemes Wall Chart Game where students stick their word cards on a board or on the wall according to the sound. So for example make three columns on the board with the past simple verbs talked, burned and wanted. These three verbs end in the sounds /t/, /d/ and /ld/ respectively. Demonstrate the three ways of saying the 'ed' verb ending and make sure students can tell the difference.

Now have a pile of past simple verbs written onto cards or pieces of paper and place these randomly in the three columns. The student's task is to match the pronunciation of the verb ending to the correct column, by saying the words, not only reading them. Simultaneously the pupil takes each word card and moves it into the correct column.

Periodically during the activity the teacher can stop the student and say that there are a certain number of verbs placed or written incorrectly on the board. The teacher does not say which verbs are incorrect, only how many are wrongly placed - the student has to figure it out and make the adjustment.

Rather than give out the rule for this let the students try to match their verbs to the correct column by saying the words repeatedly and choosing the pronunciation that seems easiest to them. Examples of words are:

/t/ liked, talked, danced, looked, dressed, watched, hoped, helped, finished, missed, kissed, washed, locked, worked

/d/ learned, played, tried, cried, lived, sewed, showed, ordered, happened, rained, played, enjoyed, screamed, opened

/Id/ wanted, floated, hated, needed, waited, visited, painted, intended

The above example is for the past simple verb 'ed' endings however use this idea with any vocabulary words where you match the word to the phoneme or matching sound on the board. Some matching sounds are the words light, bright, site and bite or the words bear, as opposed to fear, pear, as opposed to tear (to cry not to rip) and dear.

Pronunciation Feather Game

Category: Speaking - correct pronunciation for b versus p, and h.
Level: Beginner to Advanced
Materials: Something fluffy that moves when you blow on it
Age: 5 to adult
Pace: Calm

You may be familiar with this from the musical My Fair Lady. Find a feather or fluffy object that moves when you blow on it. I use pens that have fake feathers on the end, as these are readily available in my local toy store. This game works with a candle flame too but you do need to keep an eye on the candle and watch you don't ruin the Persian rug by spilling wax on it.

You will notice that if you place a fluffy object in front of your mouth and say, "bat" the fluff will not move much but if you say "pat" it is as if a gale force wind hit the fluff. The same is true to a lesser degree with "high, hate and hello" as opposed to "I, ate and yellow". Take it in turns to say words on a list you provide and give each other points for making the fluff move or not according to the word.

Pronunciation Game

Category: Speaking - correct pronunciation

Level: Beginner to Advanced
Materials: None
Age: 5 to adult
Pace: Calm

Spell out or write up a word that is frequently mispronounced. With younger children who are not reading or writing yet show a picture card. The child thinks about exactly how this word is pronounced and then says the word out loud. The teacher makes a private note as to whether this is correct or not. After you have gone through your list of words you give the correct pronunciation and award points for all correct words. You'll find that the children take great care when points are at stake! Review the words that need work and play again to see if the pupil scores higher the second time around. Play with up to ten words.

Pronunciation Hands Up

Category: Listening for phonemes and pronunciation
Level: All levels for pronunciation
Materials: None
Age: 4 to adult
Pace: Calm

This is a listening game for phonemes or pronunciation of words. The teacher repeats a word several times and then unexpectedly changes to another word using a different phoneme. Pick words that your students have difficulty with. For example a Spanish student would be likely to have trouble differentiating between ship and sheep. A French student will probably have trouble with worth and worse or earth and hearse. Japanese students will have a job with the letter r and so on.

The teacher says "lorry, lorry, lorry, lorry, lolly, lolly, lolly, lolly, lorry, lorry, lorry." When the students hear the change they raise their hands. When the change reverts back to lorry students lower their hands.

Award points for correct responses. Deduct points for hands going up before the change! As a variation have the student listen and count the number of times you say "lolly" before switching to "lorry". A big challenge is to let the students take over from you with the speaking. That certainly makes students focus on how they pronounce words.

Pronunciation Pictures

Category: Speaking
Level: Beginner to Intermediate
Materials: Pens and paper

Age: 4 to 12
Pace: Calm

Display a selection of words or pictures in contrasting pairs or groups choosing pictures of items your pupil has difficulty pronouncing. Then let the child tell you what to draw from those in the selection. The children will understand how important good pronunciation is when they see if you do draw what they said and not something different. For example if the student says "sheep" and you draw a ship then the pupil knows he did not say it right.

If you write up a selection of totally unrelated sounds the activity will not work on good pronunciation. The idea is to put up very similar sounding words so that the children have to concentrate on saying them correctly so that their partner draws the correct item.

This can be a one-off activity or an ongoing one. These pictures can go in a book or on the walls and the children can add to them any time they think of another matching word. If your child can spell he or she can write the word up alongside the picture.

Pronunciation: Silent Sounds Game

Category: Speaking
Level: Beginner to Advanced
Materials: None
Age: 6 to 12
Pace: Calm

This is a good game to highlight different vowel sounds and diphthongs, but don't take it too seriously, as it's quite hard to do, but children usually enjoy it. The teacher mouths a word silently and your pupil watches and try to guess what the sound is. For example the teacher might mouth the word bat first and let the pupil guess that, and follow it with the word pat.

Make this easier by writing up two or more columns on the board, one column for each sound you are practising so your pupil knows that you are forming one of two sounds. If using phonemes write the symbol at the top of each column, for example /ae/ for cat and /e/ for red. If not using phonemes just write up two contrasting words, one in each column. Pronounce one of the words and your pupil calls out the sound or word he or she thinks you are mouthing. You have to exaggerate to make this game possible. It's a little silly but the children enjoy it and it gives them a chance to call out different words.

GAMES Q TO R

Question and answer

Category: Speaking
Level: Beginners to Intermediate
Materials: None
Age: 3 to 12
Pace: Wake up

Throw the ball to your pupil and ask a question. Your pupil catches the ball, answers the question and throws the ball back to you, or to someone else if you have two pupils or more. Remember at first with new language to build in stages. So you always ask the question and the pupil always answers it. Then another day have the pupil do the asking while you answer. Eventually you will be able to do both.

If your young pupil cannot catch the ball roll it along the ground instead of throwing it.

This would be an excellent game to revise all sorts of question and answer forms. For intermediates allow your pupils to come up with the actual question form by telling them to ask for the time or find out someone's age, where they work, what they do and so on.

Question And Answer Lottery Match

Category: Writing and speaking
Level: Beginner to Advanced (you need to have covered several question forms for this game)
Materials: Questions
Age: 6 to 12
Pace: Wake up

Set up

Before you play ask your pupil to say as many different questions as he or she can think of. Use prompts to elicit these questions such as a clock face for "What time is it?" or a person with a suitcase and an arrow for "Where are you going?" Display these words as prompts too: what, who, where, when, have, do, how and possibly why. With intermediates revise a number of questions using arrows to indicate tense. For example the person with the suitcase and a date such as 2009 can be "Where did you go in 2009?"

How to play

Now secretly you both write out five or more questions and five answers on separate cards and keep the other person from seeing these. The answers do not need to match the questions. For example you could write the question "What time is it?" and an answer, "I'm going to London". Now you take it in turns to ask a question. For example your pupil starts by asking one of the questions he has prepared, "What time is it?" If you have an answer to that question, such as "It's three o'clock" then you must give your answer to your pupil, who now has a pair, which counts as a point. Now it is your turn to ask one of your questions.

Once you have finished asking all the questions count up to see who has the most pairs. This game is total luck so sometimes you will win and sometimes you lose. To prolong the game shuffle and redistribute any remaining cards and play a second round.

If you are doing plenty of teaching an option is for you to prepare the question and answer cards as a pack. If your students do well then play next time using many more cards and have them spread out on the floor or table with a barrier of books in the middle so that the other player's cards are not visible.

Question and Answer Treasure Hunt

Category: Reading and Speaking
Level: Beginner to Advanced
Materials: Questions and answers
Age: 6 to Adult
Pace: Calm to Wake up

Prepare a series of questions and answers on cards. Each card has either a question or an answer written on it. Place all the questions face down in a pile. Divide the answers between you and your pupil and hide them around the room. Alternatively place them around the house, clearly visible, in different rooms. Now each take a question from the pile and race around the house looking for the answer to that question. Bring the matching answer back to base and take a second question. Continue until all the questions have been matched with answers. The winner is the one with the most pairs.

If you have any other people to hand, such as a parent or family member, it is more fun if a third party distributes the answers so that neither player knows where they are.

This can be adapted to all levels of ability. For beginners a simple question and answer format is appropriate. One can use sentences and split them in half. The riddles, proverbs and metaphors included with this book can be used with advanced pupils as they require good vocabulary and can be quite cryptic.

Rapid Reaction

Category: Listening or Reading to see how words are spelled
Level: Beginners to Intermediate
Materials: Picture cards and matching word cards
Age: 6 to 12
Pace: Wake up

Spread a selection of vocabulary picture cards on the floor or table. Shuffle a pile of word cards and place them face down in the middle. Take it in turns to turn over one of the word cards in the middle. As soon as the card is turned over players race to touch the relevant picture card. This allows students to read the word and see how it is spelled. If you find that you are quicker all the time then you be the one that turns the cards over each time, as one is at a disadvantage when doing that.

A variant is shown in the video demo with Julie where we placed six cards on the table and raced to be the first to touch the one named. We took it in turns to name the cards as the person naming the card has an obvious advantage. A fun variant for this is to each have a fly swatter. It's much easier to see who gets there first with a fly swat as one can see whose is underneath!

Another variant to try out here would be for the teacher or pupil to name the card and then both players say: "Three, two, one, go!" On "Go" both players race to swat/touch the card.

Experiment also sitting at one end of the table with your hands piled on top of each other, so your hand on the bottom, then your pupil's hand, then yours again and then your pupil's. Now try the game like that. Also try by starting the other side of the room and running to the flashcards. Any slight variant makes the game different so keep using it to introduce different vocabulary without so obviously always going through the same formula.

With younger players, or less able ones, start by laying out two cards and then gradually add to them.

Language ideas

To make the game harder instead of using single word cards use whole sentences. So if one of the vocabulary cards is a tennis racket the matching sentence could; "Do you play tennis?" or "I play tennis on Saturdays". The game is more fun when it is fast, so familiarity with the sentences will speed the game up.

Recognising Tenses

Category: Listening
Level: Beginners to Intermediate
Materials: None
Age: 4 to 12
Pace: Wake up

This game is good to review several tenses and also to review two tenses while introducing one new one.

Stand about 2 metres apart so that you cannot touch each other without moving. Your pupil will listen to many sentences in different tenses. When you

110

say a sentence in the present tense the pupil moves one place to the left. When you say a sentence in the past tense he or she moves to the right and when you say a sentence in the future you have to try and touch the pupil before he can jump out of the way, or run and touch the wall where he is safe.

This can be varied as much as you like. Play with any mixture of tenses and add in extra movements such as clapping when hearing the present continuous and so on.

Once the pupil is familiar with the game a variant is for the teacher to also make the movements but sometimes deliberately making the wrong movement, which the pupil must not copy, or he loses a point (similar to the idea in Simon Says where the teacher tries to trick the other player into making a false move).

Remember and Write

Category: Writing
Level: Beginner to Advanced
Materials: Pictures or real objects
Age: 6 to 12
Pace: Calm

Display at least 12 picture cards or objects on a tray. Give yourselves a limited time to look at and memorize all the objects or pictures. Then cover them over and allow a couple of minutes for your pupil to write down as many items as he or she can remember. Play with a list of words to help pupils learn and remember spelling.

If you want to work on a target structure with this vocabulary revision game then ask the pupils to write out a set sentence containing each of the words. So if you want to practise "Do you like", use food pictures. Instead of just writing "banana" you write, "Do you like bananas?"

It is better if the pupil makes up the list of items on the tray - he or she will be better at memorising them subsequently. Alternatively make the tray up together, each putting in six items.

Note that you cannot use this game to learn spelling - only to revise it and also to revise grammar.

Roller Ball

Category: Listening

Level: Beginner
Materials: A large piece of material or cardboard and a ball
Age: 4 to 10
Pace: Calm

Pin or tape some picture cards onto a sheet. Stand at either end of the sheet and hold it taut. Next place a ball on the sheet and move the sheet in such a way that it rolls over to one of the pictures. Say the name of the picture or item and work together to make the ball roll over that picture. This might work with the side of a card board box and something like a drafts piece too. I have not tried it but it's the same idea, and might actually work better than the sheet and ball.

This is a fun coordination game where the target vocabulary is repeated frequently. The pupil may also say the word on the picture every time the ball goes over it if you want speaking skills.

Run and Touch

Category: Listening
Level: Beginner
Materials: Pictures or the things around you.
Age: 3 to 10
Pace: Calm

This is a simple game which young children enjoy. Place your pictures in different corners or parts of the room and call out an item. The children run to that picture.

As always you have the option to just name the items or use a short sentence such as "fly to the beach" or; "Can you find the beach?"

This game works particularly well for colours, clothing and objects which you have around you, because the children look and travel around the room seeking out the colour or object, which may be present in many places. For example using colours they could touch colours anywhere in the room, or being worn by someone.

When you are introducing new vocabulary throw in some different things for them to touch which they already know for revision.

Keep up a rapid pace throughout so that the pupil has no time in between listening to your commands and is constantly on the go, alert and getting lots of listening practice, thus learning the new words.

Run and Write

Category: Learning spelling
Level: Beginner to Intermediate
Materials: Lists of vocabulary or sentences.
Age: 6 upwards
Pace: Wake up

Give your pupil a list of words. Call out one of the words several times. The student has twenty seconds to find that word in the list and memorise the spelling. Give another twenty seconds for the student to run to the other side of the room and write that word out from memory. If successful in the given time award a point. Depending on your pupils you will want to modify the time limits. Allow less time for a very able pupil. A way to gauge it is to give the task once with no time limit and see how long the pupil takes. Then allow just a few seconds less than that for the game.

Use sentences too. Students hunt for a sentence you say in a reading passage from their textbooks. When found students study the sentence, memorise it and write it on the board when ready. Use the game with any grammar, tenses or vocabulary. For a list of words you may have one ready-made at the back of your textbook.

At the end check the work and if you find any errors do those words or sentences again so you finish with everything written correctly by the student.

Running Race Question and Answer

Category: Speaking
Level: Beginners to Intermediate
Materials: Pictures
Age: 3 to 12
Pace: Wake up to Excitable

Play as for Find Me where the pupil races to find a picture while you count. The pupil asks you the same question every time, such as "what are you wearing?" The teacher answers with, "I'm wearing trousers." The pupil then runs down to the pile of pictures at the end of the room and brings back the picture of trousers, before the teacher has finished counting to ten.

Language Ideas

The game can be used with as many question and answer forms as you have imagination. Here are some examples:

Clothing: What are you wearing? I'm wearing..trousers!

Past tense: Where did you go on holiday? I went to the beach

Weather: What's the weather like? It's raining.

Professions: What do you do? I'm a doctor

Telling the time: What time is it? It's one o'clock

Age and numbers: How old are you? 'I'm 10

Sports and past tense: What did you do this weekend? I played tennis

Substitute word flash cards instead of picture cards if you do not have any pictures, although using pictures is better for working with vocabulary.

Russian Roulette

Category: Speaking

Level: Beginners to Intermediate

Materials: Flashcards and a dice or coin

Age: 3 to 12

Pace: Calm

Option with preparation: Tape flashcards to the floor in a circle so there are no gaps in between the flashcards. Make a coin using thick cardboard and draw an arrow on each side pointing outwards. Spin the coin, when it falls the pupil names the flashcard the arrow is pointing at.

Option with no preparation: Another way to play is to place six flashcards in a circle on the floor but do not worry about using tape or gaps. Decide which flashcard is number one. The player whose turn it is rolls a dice and names whichever flashcard corresponds to the number rolled on the dice by counting round from flashcard number one clockwise. Use twelve flashcards and play with two dice. Another alternative is to lay out your desired number of flashcards in a circle and spin a real coin. Take it in turns to slaps your hand down on the spinning coin and then name any flashcard.

Any of the three versions above can also be played with markers. You each have markers - use any small objects such as pieces from a chess set or other board game, or failing that, small pieces of paper, blue for you and red for the pupil. When a player successfully names a flashcard he places his marker on it. As a variant when using markers, play where only one marker is allowed per card, so if a player rolls the dice and a marker is already on that card the person skips a turn. With three year old children the fewer rules you have the better as they will be happy just with the novelty of spinning the coin or placing their markers on cards, but if playing with older children some restrictions and rules can add to the fun.

Use the game for naming vocabulary or to work with grammar by forming sentences with the words.

GAMES S

Scissors Paper Stone

Category: Speaking
Level: Beginner to Advanced
Materials: None
Age: 4 to 12
Pace: Calm

Sit opposite your pupil and you both say "scissors, paper, stone". On "stone" you both make a shape with your hands as follows: a V with the index and middle finger, a fist, or a hand held out flat. The V represents scissors, which can cut the paper but are blunted by the stone. The fist represents the stone, which blunts the scissors but can be wrapped by the paper. The hand held out flat represents the paper, which can wrap the stone but is cut by the scissors. The scissors win over the paper, which wins over the stone, which wins over the scissors. On the count of three both players make and name the symbol for one of the three items.

The person losing has to do a forfeit, go first in a game, name a vocabulary flashcard, make up a sentence in English, or anything else that you feel useful or appropriate.

As a point of interest in England holding up the index and middle fingers with palm facing outwards means V for "victory". However holding up the same two fingers with the back of the hand facing outwards is an insulting gesture of the worst kind. This is exclusive to England and dates back to the wars with France when English soldiers decimated French armies with their archers. The French in response would chop off the index and middle fingers of prisoners so they could never fire a bow and arrow again. Consequently the

English soldiers would wave these two fingers arrogantly at the French to say that they could still kill them. So when playing this game be careful never to hold up your two fingers in this way when you are the scissors, but hold the fingers sideways or facing down.

Sentences

Category: Speaking
Level: Beginner to Advanced
Materials: Pictures
Age: 4 to 12
Pace: Calm

Put a pile of pictures (or better still, use real objects) in one basket or box and a pile of colours or other adjectives in another. Have the child run up to the baskets and take one item from each and make a sentence with those two words. The sentence will likely be using a prescribed form that you are practising. If a child picks out a picture of a train and the colour red he or she can say: red train, or I like red trains, or I have a red train, or this is a red train, etc. This may be adapted to any sentence. If you mix up colours and fruits you could have a blue apple and other unlikely combinations, which young children will find funny.

Shopaholics

Category: Step 4 Speaking Drill
Level: Beginner to Lower Intermediate
Materials: Picture flashcards or real items and pretend money, which can be paper, coins or any small objects
Age: 4 to 12
Pace: Wake up

In this game pupils pretend to buy things. Play with real objects if you have them, otherwise use pictures. Shoppers each have a set amount of money and must accumulate as many products as possible. The shopkeepers cannot sell anything unless correctly asked for in English. Shoppers have a time limit to buy as many items as they can.

There is a catch. At the end of the time limit your pupil draws one of the items from a hat - the item drawn represents one of the products is off and must be recalled. If your pupil has that item in the shopping basket he or she earns no points for that round. Start again. The aim is for the pupil to earn a given number of points within three rounds. I suggest one or two minutes per round, depending on whether you will be paying with real money and giving change.

Give students plenty of money so he or she has enough. If you have monopoly money that is fantastic, otherwise use pieces of paper. Young children love playing with money as it makes them feel grown up.

Use a set dialogue. For something very simple students say: "I'd like some tomatoes please", and you hand them over. For more able/advanced students make up a more realistic dialogue such as: "How much are the tomatoes? They are one pound a kilo. I'll have two kilos please. That will be two pounds. Here you are. Thank you." If you have a longer dialogue allow 2 to 3 minutes for each shopping round.

As the children will be repeating the same thing over and over this is a drill type game so accuracy is important. Swap roles giving your pupil a chance to be the shopkeeper.

Shopping List Easy Memory Game

Category: Speaking
Level: Beginner to Lower Intermediate
Materials: Optional Pictures
Age: 4 to 12
Pace: Calm

This variant can be used with relatively new vocabulary because the pupil just has to copy the teacher. Sit opposite each other. Start the game saying "one hat". Your pupil repeats this. Now add one item, "one hat, two gloves", your pupil repeats it. Add a third item and keep going for as long as possible. Play again and see if you manage to make a longer list the second time around. Use with any vocabulary.

Show Me

Category: Listening
Level: Beginners to Lower Intermediate
Materials: None
Age: 3 to 12
Pace: Wake up

This game is ideal for introducing new vocabulary. Lay out a few flashcards - starting with two or three for young children. Name the cards and ask your pupil to touch the card you name. Start slowly and gently and gradually speed up, jumping back and forth from one picture to the other, for example: spider, snake, spider, snake, spider, snake, spider, LION! The pupil will have got into a pattern of movement touching the spider and the snake and suddenly you throw in a different animal. You may also say two or more words in a row.

Variation

In this variation you show three pictures to your pupil and lay them face down on the table. Now name one of the pictures. The child must pick out that picture and show it to you, before replacing it face down again. With children aged three start this game with only two pictures. Start with less pictures rather than more – as it's easy to feed in more pictures to make it harder.

Simon Says

Category: Listening
Level: Beginners to Lower Intermediate
Materials: None
Age: 4 to Adult
Pace: Wake up

Simon says is MUCH better if you have more than one pupil. If you are teaching just one child then use it for the younger ones.

The classic version of Simon Says is as follows: The teacher starts off as Simon and gives the players instructions which they must follow, but only if Simon says so. For example:

Simon says touch your nose. (Simon touches his nose) Players must touch their nose.

Simon says touch your feet. (Simon touches his feet) All players must touch their feet.

Touch your head. (Simon touches his head) Players must not touch their head because Simon didn't say so.

Optional rules to add spice to the game: Each time your pupil successfully carries out an action defined by Simon he or she takes a step forward, the goal being to reach a given point. Each time your pupil makes a mistake he or she goes back to the beginning, and may only do this three times in one round.

Language Ideas

Obviously Simon Says is a great game to play for body parts, and once your players have got the hang of the vocabulary they can be Simon. However the language potential for Simon Says does not stop there. Here are some other examples of things that Simon can say:

Raise your left hand/Touch your right leg
Touch something blue
Touch different articles of clothing

Touch a body part of the person next to them

Jump/run/skip/stop/dance/sing/be   silent/sit   down/stand up/listen/look at the ceiling/look up/look down/look to the left/look at the floor/touch a chair/write/

Mime an animal

Mime an action such as drink a glass of water/eat an ice cream/sleep/ get dressed/ get undressed/pretend to be a model/pretend to be batman/be Spiderman

Jump on a picture - lay out pictures on the floor for the players to become familiar with or revise specific vocabulary. Simon says Jump on the train! Jump on the bus! etc.

Touch a real object - lay out objects that the players touch on Simon's instruction.

Touch the train/the car/the plane if you have toy versions of these for example, or use pictures if not.

Harder versions of Simon Says

For players with a good command of the language, and once they have got Simon Says down pat, complicate the game to keep them on their toes. In this version Simon says two things at once, for example:

Simon says raise your hand and Simon says touch your leg

The players must raise their hand and touch their leg

Simon says eat ice-cream and touch your nose

The players must eat ice cream but not touch their nose because Simon did not say so.

And here is a third, even more complicated version - you may have to rehearse being Simon for this one!

When Simon says to do something the players have to keep doing it until Simon specifically asks them to stop. In the meantime Simon continues to make other requests. For example:

Simon says touch your head

Simon says touch your shoulder and Simon says stick your tongue out

Simon says spin around and shout JUMP!

At this point the players should be spinning round with one hand on their head and the other on their shoulder, sticking their tongue out, but they should not shout JUMP! as Simon did not say to do so.

Simon then continues with: Simon says stop touching your head and rub your stomach instead

Players must stop touching their heads but should not rub their stomachs, as Simon did not say so.

Well I'm sure you get the picture. This game can really be a lot of fun and the trick is for you as Simon to keep the pace up and link the commands rapidly so your players' attention is absolutely riveted on listening to your every word!

Snap

Category: Speaking
Level: Beginners to lower intermediate
Materials: plenty of picture or word cards
Age: 3 to 12
Pace: Calm

This is the regular card game "Snap" where you have two piles of cards face down on the table. Say "ready" and each player simultaneously turns over a card. If these are the same the first person to say "Snap" wins. The winner takes all the cards that have been turned over and places them face down at the bottom of his or her pile. Continue by turning over more cards. The idea is to collect all the cards so that the other person can no longer play, although this can take ages so when you have had enough you stop the game and count up to see who has the most cards.

Instead of saying "snap" players say the word in question, either naming the picture or reading out the word. Using written words introduces spelling while picture cards revise vocabulary.

Sorting

Category: Speaking (vocabulary revision)
Level: Beginners
Materials: Pictures and boxes or bags
Age: 3 to 10
Pace: Calm

In this game your pupil will name and sort vocabulary pictures. For example give the pupil a big pile of pictures of two categories of words, such as family members and animals. Let the child pick up the pictures and tell you whether they are of a person or an animal. Alternatively have the child name the family member or animal specifically and then place the picture in the correct pile or box - a box for people and a box for animals.

For children aged three to six the idea of the boxes will add significantly to the novelty of the game. If you don't have boxes use bags, or baskets, or saucepans - anything you have to hand. If you had card board boxes such as shoe boxes and you cut a slit in the side so children posted the pictures through the slot, that's another novelty factor that they enjoy.

Another way of doing this is to scatter the pictures around the room and let the child collect one picture at a time, name it and place it in the correct box or pile. Alternatively the child makes a sentence using the word before placing it in the correct box.

Lucky Dip Idea

Another way of sorting is to place all the pictures or colours in a large box with a hole in the top, just big enough for the children to reach in. Takes it in turns at pulling out a picture, or item. The child then names the item and places it in an appropriate smaller box, or pile. So you might have colours, numbers and animals in the large box. Then you will have three separate boxes, one for all the colours, one for the numbers and one for the animals. Vary the vocabulary according to what you are revising.

Idea: Anyone pulling out a blue elephant wins all the cards in the animals box...

Spelling and Alphabet Revision

Category: Listening and speaking variants
Level: Beginners to revise the alphabet
Materials: Letters of the alphabet, either real or written
Age: 5 to 12
Pace: Calm

How to Play

Use this game for the alphabet, and also for spelling.

Give your pupil a pile of letters and spell out a word. Your pupil takes the relevant letters from the pile and form the word. With the younger children only give them a few letters to start off with, while they familiarise themselves with the concept.

To start with give out different letter combinations, such as all the consonants and the vowel A – then spell out easy words such as P A T, C A T, F A T, etc. Round two can be a letter combination of all the consonants and the vowel I, for words such as F I T, B I T, P I T etc. Repeatedly return to words already spelled and redo them, for example, cat, fat, pat, cat, sat, mat, fat and so on.

For older children give your pupil a picture card. He or she spells the word out with the letters. Keep the words simple to start with. With older or more advanced pupils, use longer words, and words with more complex spellings.

The spelling can be done as a race between you and your pupil. With siblings where you want to avoid competition do not give the children the same word to spell. The older sibling can be spelling a longer word while the younger one spells something short and repeatedly re-spells the same words.

This keeps both challenged by the task and working alongside each other but without competing.

Materials

If you do not have any real letters such as scrabble sets or fridge magnets just make them by writing one letter per piece of paper or card.

Spelling Board Game and Variants

Category: Spelling
Level: Beginner to Intermediate
Materials: Words and optional use of board games
Age: 6 to adult
Pace: Calm

Using board games for spelling

If you have some board games available you may use any one that uses dice so players can advance around the board. Your pupil rolls the dice. The teacher turns over a word card from a pile on the board without showing this to the pupil and reads out the word. Your pupil spells this word. If correct he can advance his piece around the board by the number of squares shown on the dice and have another go. If incorrect show the correct spelling but the pupil cannot move his piece that turn. Continue until one of the players makes it all the way round the board. To make it fairer In a one to one situation the teacher never rolls the dice and can only move round the board when the pupil makes an error. Or let the teacher only move two squares at a time. This gives the pupil a fighting chance of winning.

A variant to use with board games is instead of using dice use a pile of words. The player turns over a word card and spells out the letters, then moves forward the same number of spaces as there are letters in that word. That version practises saying the letters of the alphabet and seeing how words are spelled. To spell words from memory use picture cards instead.

Variant with no board game

If you do not have access to any board games or dice play this variant. Have a pile of word cards face down on the table. The teacher turns over a card and reads out the word. The pupil must spell this out and if correct, keeps the card. If incorrect the teacher keeps that card as a point. As with the board game version above the teacher never has a go but can only earn points when the pupil makes an error.

Spot the Difference

Category: Writing
Level: Beginner to Intermediate
Materials: Two similar but not identical pictures
Age: 6 to 12
Pace: Calm

Prepare in advance two identical pictures and either colour them in different colours, or make some changes to one of them. Show the first picture for a few minutes and then cover it up and show the second picture. Your pupil writes down the differences. See how many differences you find in a given time limit.

A way to obtain two similar pictures easily could be to use a web cam that is broadcasting on a website. Save the image in the morning and then again at night. The background will be the same but there will be differences in the people in the image, the time of day and what is happening. The Val d'Isère tourist office has a web cam of the slopes for example and one can spot differences in the people skiing past.

Providing gap fills as a prompt will help your pupil form sentences correctly. For example you may have drawn a picture of a cowboy, and in the second picture you draw the same cowboy but with a pink hat with a feather and some different coloured pointy boots. On the board you write: The cowboy _ _ _ wearing a _____, now he is _ _ _ _ _ _ _ _ _ a _____. The pupils should fill that in as follows: The cowboy was wearing a black hat, now he is wearing a pink hat.

GAMES T

Taboo

Category: Listening, good for revision of vocabulary
Level: Beginner to Intermediate
Materials: None
Age: 4 to 12
Pace: Wake up

Sit facing each other with your palms face up while your pupil has his or her hands face down on your palms. Tell your pupil which word, or words are taboo for the round. Now reel off a great quantity of vocabulary, or tell a story, and unexpectedly say the taboo word while trying to tap your pupil's hands. If you succeed then the pupil has a go saying vocabulary words, if able, if not continue another round in the same roles.

Talking Card Game

Category: Step 4 speaking
Group size: 2 or more
Level: Beginner to advanced
Materials: Pack of cards
Age: 5 upwards
Pace: Calm

This is a standard card game with language added. The rules of the card game are as follows: Split a pack of cards into three, a third for each player and a third placed face down in the middle. A card is turned over from the middle pile. Player A must place a card on top of this but it must follow suit so a heart may be placed on a heart. One may change suits by using a joker, or by placing the same card but in a different suit. For example a 4 of hearts may be placed on a 4 of spades and that changes the suit from spades to hearts. Players alternate, missing a turn whenever no card can be placed, until neither can place a card, at which point another card is turned up from the pile in the middle. The winner is the one with no cards left first.

So much for the rules of the game. Now for the language element. Picture cards are associated to questions. So every time a picture card is played a speaking task occurs. Attribute a theme to each suit such as describing people and things for spades, hobbies and things you like doing for hearts, things you really hate for clubs and things you would like to have for diamonds. Thus when a queen of hearts is used the player has to describe someone or something in order to be able to place the card. When a king of spades is used the player describes any hobby or thing that he or she likes doing.

This idea may be developed and it would be fun for teacher and pupil to write up a set of questions to go with each picture card. This would mean a dialogue can occur every time a picture card is used.

Use the ideas below for inspiration to make your own. These items are easily adapted to suit the level of your pupil. With advanced pupils how and why questions are good because they can elicit longer responses. If he student is involved in creating the questions he will choose topics that are of personal interest, and thus be more interested in the game.

♠Spades: Fiction

Jack – What is your favourite movie?
Queen – What is your favourite cartoon character?
King – How many sisters does Cinderella have?
Ace – What are Shrek's friends called?

♣ Clubs: Descriptions

Jack – Describe yourself
Queen – Describe your bedroom
King – Describe 'x' (x being a favourite character from a film or book)
Ace – Describe someone in your family

♥ Hearts: Things you like

Jack – Which do you prefer, summer or winter?
Queen – What things make you laugh?

King – What is your favourite food?
Ace – What is your favourite fun thing to do?

♦Diamonds: Ideals

Jack – What do you want to do when you grow up?
Queen – What would you prefer, a motorcycle or a car?
King – What would be the first thing you would cook if you were hungry?
Ace – What country would you like to visit?

The Big Freeze

Category: Listening
Group size: Minimum 2 pupils plus teacher for best results
Level: Beginner to Intermediate
Materials: None
Age: 4 to 12
Pace: Calm

Have your pupil walk around the room while you tell a story, sing a song or randomly say a number of words. The student listens intently to you and whenever you say a specified word or phrase he or she must freeze. If a pupil moves he loses a life or has to do a forfeit. For example you could say that whenever you say an item of clothing the pupil must freeze, or a type of food, or a profession, or a specific phrase. Your story can be nonsense, and it doesn't matter if the players understand all of it, or even any of it, as they are listening out for the special words. It is nice if you tell a real story, but it is not an obligation to play the game.

A variant on this is instead of freezing to clap, which allows you to keep up a faster pace instead of stopping for prolonged periods to see if your pupil is moving. For the 4 to 6s they can sit down whenever they hear the word.

For variety, tell your story or say your words in a rap rhythm, and also play a song (make sure one can actually hear the words in it though), and ask the players to listen out for certain words, so if you played Sting's "Every breath you take" you could have the players listen out for "watching, heart, baby, please, breath". With a younger audience you would want to choose songs for their age group such as Old MacDonald Had A Farm.

Spelling game

This may also be a spelling game. Say a word such as cat and then spell it out. If you spell it correctly the children keep moving, if you spell it wrong the children freeze or clap.

The Crossing

Category: Speaking
Level: Beginner to Intermediate
Materials: Picture cards
Age: 3 to 10
Pace: Wake up

This is a very easy speaking game. Each player has two pictures or pieces of paper. Line up on the starting line, the beach, and cross the ocean to the other side by stepping only on your two A4 sheets of paper. Each time you step on the paper you must name the picture on it. To cross the ocean a player has to place one piece of paper in front of himself at a time, and step on it. He then reaches round and takes the other piece of paper and places it in front of him, steps on it and so on. Players are not allowed to step in the sea!

Consider using a rule where if a player steps on the floor by accident, or does not name the picture, he or she has to take one step backwards on their paper before moving forward again. Give out new picture words to use and race again and see if you are both quicker the second time.

If your child is two and a half or three and finds this too hard then help with moving the papers while the child walks and names the pictures. Then swap over. If you want to add some excitement make it a race but a group race. Time how long it takes for the whole group to make it across the ocean.

Three cups

Category: Speaking
Level: Beginner to Lower Intermediate
Materials: 3 identical cups and some pictures
Age: 3 to 12
Pace: Calm

Use small pictures for this game, or words written on paper if you want to help with spelling. Roll up the pictures into a tube so that they fit inside a cup. Turn your cups upside down and switch them around. The object is to guess which picture is under each cup.

Start by selecting one of the cups and naming and then revealing the picture - very young children may well think it's funny if you get it wrong. You then let them have a go at guessing. They find this fun and it gives them a chance to use the same words frequently.

If you want to do more words, swap the pictures over every now and then.

In the demo of this game with Anna I wanted Anna to try to follow the cup with the fox picture. I did not have three identical cups so it was pretty easy. She preferred to play the game as a complete guessing game, where she wore a blindfold while I moved the cups, so that's what we did.

Tickle Game

Category: Listening to numbers and the alphabet, naming vocabulary
Level: Beginners
Materials: None
Age: 4 upward
Pace: Wake up

This game does numbers, the alphabet and vocabulary. Your pupil says a number and you start counting on her arm, walking up to her head and down on the other arm if necessary. When you reach the chosen number, your pupil puts his or her finger on the place you had reached and keeps it there till the end. Now you say the alphabet, walking up the arm again, over the head and down the other arm until you get to the point where you finished with the numbers, which your pupil is marking with a finger. Once there and you reached for example the letter N, your pupil has to say two or three words with the letter N but you have to tickle her while she is trying to think of them.

Tongue Twisters

Category: Speaking
Level: Intermediate to Advanced
Materials: None
Age: 6 upward
Pace: Wake up

Here are some classic tongue twisters to have fun with.

1. Give out the tongue twisters as anagrams and work out the sentences.

2. Dictate the tongue twister in a monotone with no punctuation and work out the punctuation and meaning.

3. Let your pupil make up a tongue twisters using sounds they have difficulty with. For example a tongue twister using the letters p and b would be useful for Arabic or Spanish speakers. A tongue twister with lots of 'th' sounds would challenge the French, like: Think of three thousand things that thrive on the earth. For the Japanese: Three red rabbits ran across the road.

Peter Piper picked a pick of pickled peppers, a pick of pickled peppers Peter Piper picked.

She sells seashells on the seashore.
The shells she sells are seashells.

I wish to wish the wish you wish to wish, but if you wish the wish the witch wishes, I won't wish the wish you wish to wish.

Betty bought butter but the butter was bitter, so Betty bought better butter to make the bitter butter better.

A proper copper coffee pot.

Red lorry, yellow lorry, red lorry, yellow lorry

Around the rugged rocks the ragged rascal ran.

Fuzzy Wuzzy was a bear, Fuzzy Wuzzy had no hair, Fuzzy Wuzzy wasn't very fuzzy, was he?

If a black bug bleeds black blood, what colour blood does a blue bug bleed?

It's not the cough that carries you off;
it's the coffin they carry you off in!

I saw a saw that could out saw any saw I ever saw before.

Any noise annoys an oyster but a noisy noise annoys an oyster more.

Advanced tongue twisters

Mr See Owned a saw. And Mr Soar owned a seesaw.
Now See's saw sawed Soar's seesaw before Soar saw See, which made Soar sore.
Had Soar seen See's saw before See sawed Soar's seesaw; See's saw would not have sawed Soar's seesaw.

I cannot bear to see a bear bear down upon a hare.
When bare of hair he strips the hare, right there I cry, "Forbear!"

A tree toad loved a she-toad who lived up in a tree.
He was a two-toed tree toad but a three-toed toad was she.

The two-toed tree toad tried to win the three-toed she-toad's heart,

for the two-toed tree toad loved the ground that the three-toed tree toad trod.

But the two-toed tree toad tried in vain.

He couldn't please her whim.

From her tree toad bower with her three-toed power the she-toad vetoed him.

Traffic Light

Category: Listening
Level: Beginner
Materials: None
Age: 3 to 10
Pace: Wake Up

The teacher calls out a word with a action associated to it and the pupil performs that action. So, to use the colours of the traffic light, from where this game gets its name, "green" means walk, "red" means stop dead and "yellow" means get ready. Vary the meaning of the traffic light colours according to your needs. For example red means clap, yellow means jump and green means sit down. Or use vocabulary so "lion" means walk, "bear" means stop and "panda" means sleep.

Start slowly and gradually mix up the commands faster and faster so it becomes more and more challenging. As an option children that make a mistake do a forfeit.

Treasure Hunt

Category: Speaking
Level: Lower Intermediate to Advanced
Materials: Pictures
Age: 4 to 12
Pace: Wake Up

Scatter pictures over a wide area around the room - on tables, on chairs and under things.

Read out a clue for one of the items, adapted to the age and language ability of your pupil. For example if the item is a television clues could be, "you sit in front of this at home", or "you watch it", or "home entertainment", or "a tool for communication". If the item is a watch clues could be "You wear it on your wrist. It tells the time. It's one o'clock". Use very easy clues with young children.

As soon as they hear the clue the players look around for the matching item. Give a one-minute time for your pupil to find the item that matches the clue.

True or False

Category: Listening
Level: Beginner to Lower Intermediate
Materials: None, items optional
Age: 4 to 12
Pace: Calm

You name an item or make a statement and your pupil says whether it is true or false. For example you point to a picture of an apple and say "pear", your student must say "False". You hold a pen under a chair and say "The pen is under the chair", the student must say, "True", etc.

Use more sophisticated language such as "Mary would have gone to the beach but her friends didn't invite her". If you said this while pointing to a beach the answer would be true, but if you were pointing to a picture of a building that would be false.

Twister

Category: Listening - Ideal for body parts and colours
Level: Beginner to Lower Intermediate
Materials: One Twister sheet per group (none needed for variant)
Age: 3 to 5
Pace: Wake up

This game works for all ages when played as a group. When used in a one on one situation it is only fun for very young children. You might find a Twister game in a shop, although it's a pretty old game now, however it is easy to make. Take an old sheet and paint circles on it of different colours using some kind of permanent marker pen.

For colours tell your pupil to put his right foot on red - he must keep his right foot on red for the duration of the game, now tell your player to put his left hand on blue, his knee on yellow, his head on green. A young child will find this entertainment enough. In a group each player takes it in turn and the group becomes a human tangle.

Use the twister idea for other vocabulary. Instead of using a sheet with coloured circles tape vocabulary cards to the floor. Now pupils may place one foot on the chips, a hand on the water, an ankle on the cheese and so on. You join in of course to add to the fun.

GAMES U TO Z

Using real objects

Category: Listening - presenting new vocabulary
Level: Beginners
Materials: Objects in a basket
Age: 3 to 8
Pace: Calm

Whenever it is possible or practical for you, use real objects to present new vocabulary for the first time. This helps make it more real for the young children, and especially for the three year old children.

Bring your objects in a basket and reveal them one at a time, naming them in English and placing them on the floor. Then ask your pupil to pass you each object in turn and put it back in the basket. Now let your pupil reach into the basket and pull out an item, which you name. Depending on the child you may want them to say the word at that point too.

Lay matching flashcards out on the floor. Take each real object from the basket, name it, give it to your pupil and let him or her place it on the matching picture card. Have the children repeat each word a few times and put the objects back in the basket. Then name one of the objects and the pupil pick that object out of the basket and place it on the correct flashcard.

Let your pupil pick an object out of the basket with closed eyes, then open his eyes and name the object, or you name it.

Continue with the Which One's Gone game below where you remove an object from your basket or box and the children have to say which one has gone.

Vocabulary Aim and Throw

Category: Listening
Level: Beginners to lower intermediate
Materials: Missiles such as scrunched up balls of paper or bean bags
Age: 3 to 12
Pace: Calm

Each player has a missile to throw - use soft non bouncy things such as balls of paper or beanbags. In the demonstrations of this game on Anna's video we used rolled up pairs of socks. Lay out some vocabulary pictures, well spread about on the floor and make a start line. Take it in turns to aim at the pictures. If a player hits a picture then he keeps it as a point.

With Anna we played with pictures spread on the floor. I told her which animal to aim at, if she hit it she kept the picture. Then she told me which one to aim at. On the video I made Anna's start line closer to the pictures than mine, and I managed the game, by moving the pictures closer to her, so that she won.

In the variant with Julie we throw the rolled up socks backwards through our legs and try to hit the pictures which are stuck on a window.

Speaking variant

Another way to play this is to have a bin or hoop to aim at. In order to have a go at throwing the bean bag in the bin the child must first answer your question or name a flashcard you show. Boys will be keen on this game as they often love throwing things.

Vocabulary Clapping

Category: Listening
Level: Beginners to lower intermediate
Materials: None
Age: 3 to 12
Pace: Calm

This is a good way to revise a lot of vocabulary you have taught during the term or previous lessons. Tell your pupil to clap once when you name an item of food and twice when you name a drink. Use this idea with any action if you want variety, and with any types of vocabulary. For example have the children clap once when you name a mode of transport and twice when you name an item of clothing.

A variation is to have the children clap when you name an item of clothing and be silent when you name any word which is not an item of clothing.

What am I?

Category: Speaking
Level: Intermediate to Advanced
Materials: Clothes pegs or sticky tape
Age: 8 to 12
Pace: Wake up

Cut out some product advertisements. Choose items children like such as Coke, Snickers, a teen magazine, KFC, Mac Donald's and M&Ms, or branch out into people and use sporting celebrities, cartoon characters or famous people.

Pick out a product or famous person. Either do this by selecting from a pile of pictures or think someone up. Above all make sure you pick something or someone that your pupil relates to and knows of. Your pupil now has to ask you questions in order to guess who or what you are. Pupils can ask any question at all as long as the answer given is a yes or a no. Then swap over and you guess the person or thing that your pupil is.

This game is demanding in terms of vocabulary so do not use it with beginners.

An interesting twist to this game, for advanced or older students is first for the teacher to ask a general knowledge question to the pupil, such as, "What is the name of Spiderman's girlfriend?" Answer: Mary Jane. For adults interested in art a question might be: "Who sculpted The Thinker?" Answer Rodin. If the pupil answers the general knowledge question he has the right to ask a direct question about the thing or person he is trying to guess. This is fantastic for general knowledge, general vocabulary and language. Be sure to ask general knowledge questions that fall within the sphere of what should be common knowledge, such as capital cities, names of oceans, historic people and dates, inventors, artists and musicians, also film stars, music and so on.

What is hiding in my pocket?

Category: Listening or Speaking
Level: Beginner
Materials: Items or pictures
Age: 3 to 9
Pace: Calm

Hide some real items in your clothing, in your hair, your shoes, your socks, in pockets, up a sleeve or a trouser leg, etc. Then you gradually produce each item saying; What is hiding in my pocket? or What is hiding in my sock? and you bring out the item which you or your pupil names.

A fun variation is to use coloured scarves or coloured objects. You hide the scarves all about you, in your boots, under your hat, up a trouser leg, in your pockets, etc. It helps if you put on your coat or a couple of jackets so you have plenty of pockets. Then like a magician you materialise the coloured scarves or objects. This is good for naming clothing, colours, prepositions, or asking questions. Then hide the scarves about your pupil and let them have a go as the magician.

What Time is it Mr Wolf?

Category: Speaking - telling the time and / or meal times
Level: Beginners to Lower Intermediate
Materials: None
Age: 4 to 6
Pace: Lively

The teacher/wolf walks slowly ahead with the pupil following behind. The pupil asks "What's the time Mr Wolf?" Mr Wolf replies "It's one o'clock" (or whatever time he likes). The pupil repeats the question until Mr Wolf replies, "It's dinner time!" At this point Mr Wolf turns round and tries to catch the pupil, who has to run to touch a wall for safety.

Mr Wolf can also call out breakfast time, lunchtime, teatime, supper time, and even elevenses, (a British custom of coffee or tea and biscuits around 11am). Whenever Mr Wolf calls out a time involving eating he turns and chases the pupil.

If your pupil is very young and is scared of the idea of a wolf then play what time is it Mummy?

Which One Has Gone?

Category: Speaking - naming vocabulary
Level: Beginners to Lower Intermediate
Materials: A set of picture cards or objects
Age: 4 to 12
Pace: Wake up

Put up a set of picture cards on the table and ask your pupil to close his eyes. To prevent cheating you could ask him to fold his arms on the desks and put his heads on his arms so there is no way he can see what you are doing. Take away one of the cards on the table and say, 'which one has gone?"

or, "open your eyes!" When the pupil hears this question he looks up and has five seconds to name the missing picture.

Take away more than one picture at a time if you wish, or make the task harder for older children by moving the pictures around in between goes. With four year old children start with two pictures only and gradually add to it.

Whose Shadow is it?

Category: Speaking
Level: Beginners to Lower Intermediate
Materials: A sheet and a light, a dark room
Age: 3 to 12
Pace: Wake up

Children love this! Hang a sheet up, or drape one over a couple of chairs. Turn all the lights out except for a light or torch behind the sheet. Sit your pupil in front of the sheet and you go behind. Now you make an action and your pupil has to guess what you are doing. Or make a shape of an object in a given theme, such as food, or an animal, or a type of transport, or a profession. Then swap over and let your pupil have a go acting while you call out plenty of words trying to guess. To help them think up what to act an idea is to have a bunch of picture cards or objects behind the sheet as prompts. Many young children have a job thinking up what to act on their own, at least if they are not used to thinking for themselves.

Who Wants to Be a Millionaire Adaptation

Category: Speaking
Level: Beginner to Intermediate
Materials: None
Age: 4 to Adult
Pace: Calm

Draw a column on the board with 5 squares in each. Ask your pupil a question - any type of question according to what you are working on. This could be something like, "Do you like milk?" If your pupil replies, "Yes I do" that is a correct answer (grammatically), so your pupil earns a cross in the lowest square and progresses to the next square up. continue with the second question. Your student has to get five correct answers in a row to win the million/prize. Any error means the pupil goes back to square one again.

With beginners ask easy questions such as: "What is your name?" With four and five year olds ask the same questions repeatedly, (where is she from? where are they from? where are you from?) this is an excellent excuse to drill.

The questions do not need to be general knowledge as you are testing English here.

Write It Up

Category: Writing
Level: Beginner to Advanced
Materials: Board and pens
Age: 6 to 12
Pace: Wake up

This is a revision game. Either use this to revise a variety of vocabulary themes or sentence structures or use it as a drill for a single type of sentence, such as, "I like running. I like eating. I like going to the cinema."

Call out a word or a sentence. Your pupil jumps up, runs over to a big sheet of paper stuck on the wall or on the floor and writes that word up before you have counted to ten. If correct he earns a point. The pupil returns to the start point and is ready to run on hearing the next word or sentence.

With beginners writing up sentences in this way may be too ambitious, so use single words instead.

Writing Race

Category: Writing
Level: Beginner to Advanced
Materials: Pens or pencils and paper
Age: 6 to 12
Pace: Wake up

Here is an easy, fun writing game. This game is to be played once your students are familiar with the vocabulary and sentences and is particularly good for practising specific grammatical points or spelling. It adds a really fun twist to worksheets!

You and your pupil each have a pencil, a worksheet and a blank piece of paper. On the word go your pupil runs to the worksheet and fills in the blank/s for the first item on the worksheet. He or she then runs back to the blank piece of paper and writes the item out in full there. This may be the whole sentence or just the words that went into the blanks on the worksheet. The pencils stay with the worksheets so there is no running with them.

As soon as the first child reaches the blank piece of paper the teacher can run to the worksheet and fill in the second item, leave the pencil on the desk and run to the blank piece of paper. The first child should have finished writing out the item by now, and runs back to the worksheet to do the third item. Here is a concrete example of how that works. Using a worksheet for a/an the pupil runs to the worksheet and fills in item 1, in this case 'an' before elephant. The child then runs back to the blank piece of paper and writes out 'an elephant', while the teacher runs to the worksheet and fills out item 2, 'a' before ball, and so on.

A variant is to have two worksheets instead of a blank piece of paper - either identical for reinforcing newly learned things, or different ones for revising a greater number of items. When the worksheets are all filled up the game is over. For marking let the pupil mark things, ticking where correct. Rather than correcting the child yourself say that something is wrong with that item and let the child have a chance to spot the error alone. This is better from a learning point of view, and also for self-esteem.

This game lends itself to any language as long as it is short - being a writing race it isn't practical to have great long sentences to write out. However if you use 2 worksheets and just do fill in the blanks then the sentences can be as long as you like. If you wanted to reinforce some spelling then you could have one worksheet which the pupil runs to, memorizes the first word, runs back to the blank piece of paper and writes that word down from memory while the teacher runs to the worksheet to memorize the second word, and so on. You could also use that idea for very short sentences or vocabulary.

A spelling idea is to use a worksheet with pictures only. The child looks at the first picture, runs back to the blank piece of paper and writes down the word. Use any language with fill in the blanks such as question forms, verb endings, parts of verbs, vocabulary, pronouns.

www.teachingenglishgames.com/games/Writing_Race_Worksheets.htm

Zambezi River

Category: Speaking
Level: Beginner to Intermediate
Materials: Picture flashcards
Age: 4 to 10
Pace: Wake up

The Zambezi is a river that flows over the Victoria Falls and below the rapids it is infested with crocodiles! The pupil/s have to get across the river without being eaten by the crocodiles. They do this by jumping from rock to rock or picture to picture and naming the pictures as they go. They have to name the picture, or say the sentence or question about the picture in order to carry onto the next rock, and finally to safety.

Language can be simple vocabulary to sentences or questions. For example all the players ask in unison "Where are you going?" and the player crossing the Zambezi says, "I'm going to the beach, I'm going to the circus, I'm going to the zoo", as he or she steps on pictures of the beach, the circus and the zoo.

With younger children they can be quite perturbed by the prospect of being eaten by the crocodile, which is real in their imagination, and therefore I never eat four year olds, or allow them to be eaten by the crocodile (the teacher). I have even seen 9 years olds on the verge of tears at the prospect of being eaten, but I have seen other 6 years old children deliberately get the word wrong just so that they can be eaten. Be sensitive to each individual - you don't want him or her in tears. How you go about eating your players depends on whether you are in a formal teaching situation, and how relaxed you are with your students - I leave it to your imagination!

RHYMES AND FINGER PLAYS

Rhymes are excellent for confidence and fluency, and for allowing syntax and grammar to be absorbed subconsciously. Children also love them, and they give an opportunity to use and see some of the words they have learned in the context of sentences, which is satisfying. Use rhymes with sophisticated tenses and language right from beginners aged three. First you teach some of the vocabulary found in the rhyme with games, and then you introduce the rhyme. Pupils will be satisfied to recognise some of the words, and with repetition, and coming back to it at the next session, perhaps using the same rhyme in a different game or setting, you will find that they will learn it over time.

Use miming with rhymes and songs whenever possible, especially with the young ones. Make up actions yourself, and ask the class for ideas for actions - you'll get some good ideas that way!

Eeny Meeny Miny Mo

Eeny Meeny Miney Mo
Catch a piglet by its toe
If it squeals let it go
Eeny meeny miney mo
O U T spells out so out you must go

Use that rhyme in a circle counting round the group as you all say the rhyme. Whichever child is out has to name a picture card or stand up and do a forfeit. That child stays in the circle but if picked again must pass the forfeit or task to another child who has not yet been picked. That way everyone gets a go and no one is ever out.

Family members

Start with the thumb and work round the fingers.
This is daddy, he's quite small.
This is mummy, she's quite tall.
This is brother, he is taller.
This is sister, she is smaller.
And this is baby,
He is tiny,
And he's fast asleep, shhhhhhh. (forefinger on lips)
Goodnight (whisper)

Five Naughty Monkeys - finger poem

The children start by holding up five fingers and then four, three, two, one and none as you say the rhyme together.
Five naughty monkeys sitting up on high,
One naughty monkey said good bye.
Four naughty monkeys sitting up on high,
One naughty monkey said good bye.
Three naughty monkeys sitting up on high,
One naughty monkey said good bye.
Two naughty monkeys sitting up on high,
One naughty monkey said good bye.
One naughty monkey sitting up on high,
This little monkey said good bye!
On another occasion add in this second verse:
One little monkey said hello,
One little monkey sitting down below
One little monkey said hello
Two little monkeys sitting down below.
One little monkey said hello
Three little monkeys sitting down below
One little monkey said hello
Four little monkeys sitting down below
One little monkey said hello
Five little monkeys sitting down below

It dip doo

A rhyme to select or eliminate someone. For example use this to decide who goes first in a game.

It dip doo

The cat's got the flu
The dog's got the chicken pox
Out goes you

Jelly in the dish
Jelly in the dish
Jelly in the dish
Wibble wobble wibble wobble
Jelly in the dish

Little Tom Thumb

Hide your thumb in your fist and say the rhyme. When you say, out you come, pop your thumb up. Say the rhyme with the children and have them copy.

Hello, hello,
Little Tom Thumb
Little Tom Thumb
Out you come!

This Little Piggy

Start with the thumb and move round the fingers. With the last little piggy make your hand run off somewhere, or you could pick a child to tickle.

This little piggy went to market.
This little piggy stayed at home.
This little piggy had roast beef.
This little piggy had none.
And this little piggy went wee wee wee wee all the way home.

Two Little Blackbirds

Make some relevant gestures with this rhyme.

Give the children two little black tissues or pieces of folded card to be the blackbirds, and use a sheet to be a wall that the birds can sit on. Then one child can go behind the wall at a time and do the actions while all the children say the rhyme together. This is a nice little thing to include in a show to parents and other children.

Two little blackbirds sitting on a wall,
One's called Peter, one's called Paul.
Fly away Peter, fly away Paul.
Come back Peter, come back Paul.

Three Blind Mice

Three blind mice
Three blind mice
See how they run
See how they run
They all ran off to the farmer's wife
Who cut off their tails with a carving knife
The three blind mice

I Like Coffee

I like coffee
I like tea
I like the boys
and the boys like me
Yes
No
Maybe so
Yes
No
Maybe so . . .

One Banana

One banana, two bananas, three bananas, four
Five bananas, six bananas, seven bananas, more

Hickory Dickory Dock

Hickory dickory dock
The mouse ran up the clock
The clock struck one
The mouse ran down
Hickory dickory dock

One Two, Buckle My Shoe

One two
Buckle my shoe
Three four
Knock on the door
Five Six
Pick up sticks

Seven eight
Lay them straight
Nine ten
Big fat hen

Porridge In A Pot

Porridge in a pot, porridge in a pot,
Hubble bubble, hubble bubble, hot, hot, hot!

Milk in a mug, milk in a mug,
Drink it up; drink it up, glug, glug, glug!

Ickle Ockle

Ickle ockle blue bockle
Fishes in the sea
If you want a pretty maid
Please choose me.

Humpty Dumpty

Humpty Dumpty sat on a wall
Humpty Dumpty had a great fall
All the king's horses and all the king's men
Couldn't put Humpty together again.

Handy Pandy

Handy Pandy Jack a Dandy
Loved plum cake and sugar candy.
He went into the baker's shop.
Then out he came, hop, hop, hop.

Hey Diddle Diddle, the Cat and the Fiddle

Hey diddle diddle, the cat and the fiddle,
The cow jumped over the moon.
The little dog laughed to see such fun,
And the dish ran away with the spoon.

Sally Goes Round The Sun

Sally goes round the sun,

Sally goes round the moon,
Sally goes round the chimney pots
On a Saturday afternoon

RIDDLES

Bearing in mind that most of these involve a play on words and good vocabulary they are best for intermediate levels. Use these with adults too - some of them are pretty good!

Why did the chicken cross the road? Because it wanted to get to the other side.

Can giraffes have babies? No, they can only have giraffes.

What does a house wear? Address

What did the sock say to the foot? You're putting me on.

How do rabbits travel? By Hare plane.

What shoes should you wear when you basement is flooded? Pumps.

What kind of ties can't you wear? Railroad ties.

Why are potatoes good detectives? Because they always keep their eyes peeled.

Why was the belt arrested? For holding up the pants.

What kind of eyeglasses do spies wear? Spy-focals.

What do you get when you saw a comedian in two? A half-wit.

When is it dangerous to play cards? When the joker is wild.

What does the invisible man drink at snack time? Evaporated milk.

What kind of soda must you not drink? Baking soda.

What part of your body has the most rhythm? Your eardrums.

How does mother earth fish? With North and South poles.

Where is the ocean the deepest? On the bottom.

Where is the best place to see a man-eating fish? In a seafood restaurant.

What do whales like to chew? Blubber gum.

What did the beach say when the tide came in? Long time no sea.

What did one potato chip say to the other? Shall we go for a dip?

What did the chocolate bar say to the lollipop? Hello sucker.

How does a king open a door? With a monarchy.

What do you need to spot an iceberg 20 miles away? Good eyesight!

What did the dog say to the little child pulling his tail? That is the end of me.

What horse never goes out in the daytime? A night mare.

Where do animals go when they lose their tails? To a retail store.

What is the best year for a kangaroo? A leap year
Something Silly
Q1. How do you put a giraffe into a refrigerator?
Open the refrigerator, put in the giraffe and close the door.
This question tests whether you tend to do simple things in an overly complicated way.

Q2. How do you put an elephant into a refrigerator?

Wrong
Open the refrigerator, put in the elephant, and close the refrigerator.

Correct
Open the refrigerator, take out the giraffe, put in the elephant and close the door.

Q3. The Lion King is hosting an animal conference. All the animals attend except one. Which animal does not attend?

The Elephant, since it is still in the refrigerator.

Q4. There is a river you must cross but it is inhabited by crocodiles. How do you manage it?

You swim across. All the crocodiles are attending the Animal Meeting.

PROVERBS

A bird in the hand is worth two in the bush
A friend in need is a friend indeed
A miss is as good as a mile
A penny saved is a penny earned
A rolling stone gathers no moss
A stitch in time saves nine
A watched pot never boils
A word to the wise is sufficient
Absence makes the heart grow fonder
Actions speak louder than words
All roads lead to Rome
All that glitters is not gold
An apple a day keeps the doctor away
April showers bring May flowers
Beggars can't be choosers
Birds of a feather flock together
Blood is thicker than water
Don't count your chickens until they're hatched
There's no use crying over spilt milk
Every cloud has a silver lining
Familiarity breeds contempt
Half a loaf is better than none
Handsome is as handsome does
Heaven helps those who help themselves
Honesty is the best policy
Horses for courses

Let sleeping dogs lie
Look before you leap
Make hay while the sun shines
Necessity is the mother of invention
One man's meat is another's man's poison
Out of the frying pan, into the fire
Practice makes perfect
Rome wasn't built in a day
Strike while the iron is hot
The early bird catches the worm
The pen is mightier than the sword
There's no place like home

CURRICULUM

Leave the alphabet for later. It's abstract and does not appeal much to young children. I recommend teaching some fun vocabulary themes to start out with and then gradually introducing the alphabet five to six letters at a time, mixed in with other vocabulary and themes.

If you have my 30 Fun ESL Role-Plays and Skits For Children, available on Amazon and on http://www.teachingenglishgames.com/eslplays.htm then you may simply follow that as a suggested curriculum. That is ideal for ages 4 to 12.

Likewise if you have a child or pupil who is between 3 to 5/6 then the preschool stories are designed to be followed as a curriculum. There are twenty stories in total.

As a general outline here are some vocabulary themes to that are either useful or fun for children.

1. Teach plain vocabulary words first

2. Incorporate those known vocabulary words into sentences to teach grammar.

3. Practise and revise constantly!!!!!!!!!

Use these suggested themes in any order, with the language you like. My ideas are suggestions of the most obvious things that come to mind for me.

1. Greetings - names, hello, goodbye, how are you?

2. Animals - good for using with descriptions and comparatives

3. Colours - later combine with descriptions for word order

4. Food - good for using with I like/I don't like. Would you like some? Yes please/No thank you. Fruits, vegetables, main meals, desserts, drinks, snacks

5. Family and friends - good for My name is, his name is etc. Descriptions of people.

6. Body parts - good for at the doctor role play and bandages

7. Clothing - good for What are you wearing? I'm wearing (present continuous)

8. Feelings - good for the verb "to be"

9. Sports and hobbies - good for I like tennis, I am playing tennis + miming, Do you play tennis? Yes I do, no I don't (present tense)

10. Furniture and rooms of the house - good for prepositions and directions, where is? and There is/There are

11. Numbers - good for use with How much is? These don't need teaching in a separate lesson but can be done through constant repetition of counting up your points or cards during games. You do all the counting at first while the pupil listens, then in the next lesson you count and your pupil repeats each number after you, and eventually your pupil will join in with you while you count. The final stage is for the child to do all the counting alone.

12. Countries - good for Where do you live? Where is?

13. Professions - good for I'm a/he's a (verb to be)

14. Places (beach, shops, cinema, country, town) - good for Where are you going at the weekend? (Future) or where have you been? / where did you go last summer?

15. Toys and items your child is into

16. Alphabet and Phonics

17. Daily routine and actions - (any tense); What you do every day (present), miming actions (what are you doing? I'm ...), what you did yesterday (past perfect)

18. The Weather and the Seasons

19. Days of the Week - good for present tense and daily routine

20. Months of the Year

21. Telling The Time (once your child knows how to do this in his or her native language)

22. Prepositions

23. Directions and asking the way

24. Transport - adjectives, miming, booking tickets role-plays, Can you drive/fly a plane?

25. Verbs – actions, commands, daily routine

26. Shapes

27. Opposites

28. School and the classroom

29. Nature and flowers

30. Instruments and music

31. Birthdays, Christmas, Easter, Valentine's Day, Halloween, Bonfire Night, Pancake Day, summer holidays, winter holidays...

Once you have taught all these if you find it impossible to think up what to teach yourself I recommend getting hold of an English grammar book, such as the one by Michael Swan, Practical English Usage, and get inspired from that! All the best with your teaching! It's very rewarding so do get started right away, even if if you play one game a day that's already going to make such a difference to your child!

ANNA STRUCTURED LESSON VIDEO COMMENTARY

A lesson to teach: lion, fox, cat, bird, snake, spider, ant and I'm hungry.

Anna is six and this is my second lesson with her. In bold you have the name of the game as it appears in this book of games. Then you have the position on the video where you will find that game in case you want to fast forward or just watch a particular game for a refresher. This also shows you the length of time I spent on a particular game before changing. This is not set in stone and by observing your pupil you know whether it's time to change or whether to continue playing. There follows notes on the teaching process shown. The rules of the game are not explained in the commentary as you'll find that under the game itself, which appears in this book in alphabetical order.

This lesson may be viewed online by book owners here:
http://www.homeenglishteacher.com/video/anna.html

1. Show Me: (0:00) Listening game to introduce new vocabulary. Notice how I start with three animals and feed more in up to five. When I strung three animals together "spider, snake, cat" that was going too fast. I had only just introduced the cat. So I had to help her by saying them individually again and then backing off and making it simpler.

2. Jump The Line: (2:17) Listening game to continue working with the vocabulary and introduce two more new words. As we set up the game I talk to her in English, although she can't understand a thing. Don't follow my example there as it's best not to chat too much like that but stick to repeating the same sentences. When I say "stand up" Anna understands as I gesture to her. That's the way to use extra English in the lessons outside of the target vocabulary, not by chatting away. Then I demonstrate the game but Anna does not quite understand it immediately so to save time I tell her the rules of the game in French. If you are a teacher and you don't speak the native language continue to demonstrate until your pupil catches on to what to do.

As I saw that Anna could not handle the three words in a row in the previous game I go back to doing single animals at the start of this game and only after a while string two together. Then I introduce two new words, lion and ant. The first few times I say these words I have to mime the animal as Anna cannot remember what they are. This kind of game uses TPR - total physical response - that's just a fancy way of saying that the pupils move and use their bodies and this helps them learn quicker.

Being positive: when Anna makes a mistake and jumps on the fox and snake instead of the spider and the snake I don't say, "no". Instead I say "snake is good, and the spider?" This way Anna does not hear a negative word, instead I focus on the part she got right before giving her another chance to get the spider right too.

3. Find Me: (5:17) More listening practice. I have not hidden the cards here, just spread them about in plain view. Notice how I string out the counting when Anna brings me the fox instead of the spider, and help her get the correct picture by miming. She ALWAYS gets back in time with the correct picture. I count quite fast to give the game a bit of excitement. It would have been better to have Anna play this barefoot as she might have slipped on the tiles with her socks on.

4. Vocabulary Aim and Throw: (7:04) See how we are using rolled up socks to play and a skipping rope - with all these games use things you have to hand in your house. An imaginary line is acceptable if you are short of any kind of prop, or you are a teacher and you do not want to show up to the lesson with a suitcase. Having said that props do add to the fun and novelty, especially for the younger children. Anna throws the sock from closer so it's easier for her. That's a way to have a genuine competition and still lose! See how the animals I get her to aim at are really close to her so she's more likely to hit them.

Then I ask her which animal I should aim at - this is the first time she has been asked to say the words, and it's done naturally in the context of a game, so she does not feel pressure or the spot light, or that she is being forced to repeat words pointlessly, just for the sake of saying them. This is a key point with the games, they provide a meaningful context in which to use the language. Anna HAS to say the words in order to play. She says "snake" with a funny pronunciation so I repeat it a couple of times, but without saying "no, say it like this..." I just repeat it so she can hear it said correctly again.

She's so delighted when I miss! When I say "yes or no?" I have not taught her those words yet but she knows what I mean from the context and says "no". Notice how she did not say "non" in French - that shows how the "extra" language goes in bit by bit as part of the process. When I say, "which one? which animal?" again she knows what I mean from the context and shows her understanding by saying "fox". So be careful not to chat away, you'll get better results with fewer words used in context with gestures to clarify meaning.

After a while I move the pictures remaining closer so the game does not drag on forever and so Anna will have success aiming at the pictures. See how I help her when I say "cat or bird, cat or bird?" That's a reminder to her of those words so she can say one of them. She wants to see who has won so we count up our cards.

5. Speaking exercize: (12:37) This is not a game. Now we spend a few minutes concentrating on saying the words. Notice how I don't go through all seven animals in a row but show two, then go back to the first one, on to a third, back to the second and so on. This repetition helps your pupil remember. If you go straight through all seven words in a row, chances are you'll have to help the pupil every time over and over again. When Anna needs help notice how I start by giving her the beginning of the word.

6. Miming Games: (14:12) Here we take it in turns to imitate the animals and guess which one it is. I left the pictures out as prompts and that helps a lot as Anna can look at the pictures and decide which one to mime. (My husband who is on the camera can't help putting in his contribution here and asking for a "little monkey", because that's what he calls his niece, but she's not too keen on the nickname).

7. Listen: (16:07) I went a bit fast at the start of this game pretending to chase Anna when I was saying an animal and it fooled her repeatedly. What I should have done is play more simply for a few goes, just repeating the animals without pretending to chase her. Then once she had the hang of it I could add in that extra element. Notice how when I say "I'm hungry" I make sure that she is nearer the tree than I am. She wants a turn too so the first time I run really slowly and don't let her catch me. After that I let her catch me but make it seem as if I really could not get away. If we hadn't been filming I would have played this for longer with her.

8. Diving for Treasure: (18:31) This is another listening game. In a real lesson I'd most likely continue with speaking games but I wanted to demo plenty of games for you. Here Anna has to dive to the bottom of the ocean to save the animals without breathing. After seeing how easily she did it for the first animal I gave her a longer route to run to make it more of a challenge.

9. Speaking exercize: (21.30) We go through the animals one more time, notice how much better Anna does them this time than ten minutes earlier. You may be surprised at just how long it takes, but what I'm going for is to make the pupil really remember these words and be confident saying them, and pronouncing them well. As this is Anna's first exposure to English other than some counting it's normal for her to need all this repetition. If you do sessions regularly you will find that the pace of learning increases substantially as the child gets used to hearing and saying English phonemes (sounds) that make up words. As you introduce new vocabulary themes and language it's always the same SOUNDS that return.

10. Getting Warmer / Hide And Seek: (21.55) This is a hide and seek game. Anna introduces the "getting warmer" part of it in French when I need help finding the flashcards. So this is a simplified version or variant of the game. There are umpteen ways to vary the games and it's good to play them differently to keep things fresh. Once you have been using the games for a while ideas will come to you on how to vary them, and your pupil or child will most likely have ideas to contribute, seeing as children are experts at playing.

When Anna finds the ant she says "and". I don't correct her at this point. I don't always correct everything as it can be very discouraging. If you've ever tried to speak a foreign language you might know what I mean when I say that being constantly interrupted and corrected can be pretty perturbing. So sometimes it's best to let things flow and you have to pick another moment to make a correction. I sort out that and-ant mistake later on. When Anna is counting up the cards the first time notice how she hesitates on "four" but that I don't jump in with it - I give her the space and time to think and sure enough she does think of the number on her own. Obviously you don't want it to be like "Who wants to be a millionaire" where they sit there for AGES not saying anything, but just don't be jumping in on them the whole time either.

Now Anna wants to hide them - that was not part of my lesson plan but I'm not going to deny her a turn, and Anna is the sort of child who likes to be in charge and have a turn at everything!

11. Fishing: (28.10) See how at the beginning Anna blows on the pictures - this is obviously a game she has played before and bingo, there's an example of a new game that your pupil has just given you, so be on the look out for that sort of thing while you are teaching. At first Anna thinks she has to blow not suck on the straw. Once we get that figured out she still have trouble - I let her keep trying because I've played this game with four year old children and I know it's within the capacity of a six year old child. I think it might be too hard for a three year old, and therefore frustrating, so I'd only use it from age four up. I cut a little bit of the film here as Anna keeps trying to suck up the animals. Eventually I say to Anna that she can keep the pieces of paper with the animals on and the straw and practise, but in fact she picks it up again and this time she is successful. So in short, let your child persevere, and if he or she fails try again in another session. Eventually your pupil will be able to do it.

12. Biscuit Tin: (31.22) Demonstrate first, then play. I incorporated "Getting Warmer" into this since Anna had introduced the idea herself during the hide and seek game. Watch out to place the tin quietly, or if possible silently, as otherwise it's a dead give away as to where it is. You could also use this game to give directions such as left, right, start, stop and so on.

13. Clapping Games: (34.30) At first I let Anna show me the clapping she's been doing with her sister counting. Notice how she misses out the number five the first time but I don't interrupt her and the second time she counts to ten she gets it right. That's proof that jumping in and correcting at every little mistake is not necessary.

Then we have a go at repeating the animals and adding one each time. I explain it very badly at first and it's completely my fault that the game is slow to get going. Going to four animals in a row was too much for Anna so an option is to do three words then go back to one again and repeat with the same words before adding a fourth, or go back to one and use three different nouns.

14. Stepping Stones: (36:47) See how Anna slips on the flashcard and chooses to remove her socks - anticipate this to avoid a potential accident (unlike me in the demo)! Anna is not so good at naming them now because she's been going for 45 minutes by this time and we should either have a break or call it a day. I wanted to show you a few more games so we carried on anyway, but you can see that her concentration is fading, so I'm prompting her by giving her the sound that starts the word. Then we make it different by having her do it backwards. Anna gets involved arranging the flashcards.

15. Three Cups: (39:04) Anna has another game in mind but I insist on giving her my version, where she tries to follow a specific cup. We do that with the fox and she finds it easily because I did not have three identical cups. This is a good idea with a three year old - play with two cups the same and one different so it's an easier task to keep a track of the cups, and move them slower. With children Anna's age you need three cups the same, and you need to move them pretty fast to make the game a challenge. Then Anna wants to play her version anyway, (at 48:25) where she does not look and it's based on luck, so we do that too. Notice how she finally gets the "ant" pronunciation just right with the "t" at the end.

16. A Story: (42:23) Now I tell Anna a short story, just so I could demo it for you – but I have to do it pretty quickly, and cutting much of the dialogue because Anna needs a break now. This story is part of a series of twenty stories available separately to these games and suitable for ages 3 to 5 (possibly from 2 they are OK too). Anna is at the upper age limit for these stories. The "I'm Hungry" phrase comes in that I taught Anna earlier on in the "Listen" game. After all the animals have been eaten the lion gets hiccups and the animals comes out again.

JULIE STRUCTURED LESSON VIDEO COMMENTARY

A lesson to teach: Present perfect: I've forgotten. Possessive pronoun: my. Nouns: hat, coat, gloves, keys, bag, sunglasses. Phrases: Are you ready? Yes. Are you sure?

I do recommend you read the commentary for the lesson with Anna before reading this as teaching tips mentioned there will not be repeated here so as not to become monotonous.

Julie is 12 and is learning English at school. She spent about six years at primary school learning colours over and over again and "my name is Julie". In her first year at secondary school the pace has suddenly changed and at first Julie was lost, but two lessons with me and she's top of the class. The language taught in this lesson is all new except for "sunglasses", which she already knew.

This lesson may be viewed online by book owners here:

http://www.homeenglishteacher.com/video/julie_ready.html

1. Present the vocabulary: (0:00) Because Julie is already 12 and is learning English in school I get her to say the words right away, unlike in the lesson with Anna where English sounds are pretty much totally new to her. We spend 22 seconds only on the words as Julie picks things up quickly and I think she's ready to start the first game.

2. Rapid Reaction: (0:26) This does work better with more people but it's still an acceptable game with two. You may not be able to tell but actually I'm being deliberately slow at first, as the person speaking has such an advantage. Still I'm not going be slow every time as if Julie thinks I'm faking the game it'll lose all interest for her. When we start alternating saying the words and awarding points to ourselves I tip the balance in Julie's favour by picking words that are closer to her than they are to me.

3. Mystery Bag: (2:42) This is a cross between Blindfold Guessing game and Mystery Bag. It just goes to show that from a base number of games you will soon be inventing an unlimited number of variants once you get started. This is a speaking game to give Julie more opportunity to say the new words. Notice how I give her the keys and the coat several times as she had trouble with those two words.

4. Which One's Gone?: (4:07) A fun game for more speaking which also gets those brain cells tingling as your pupil has to notice which item or picture is missing. See how I move several items but don't necessarily take them out - that's a decoy. You see Julie can hear the object being moved, whether it's paper or keys, or a big item like a coat, she'll hear the air moving. So I make a noise with the hat flashcard but actually take the gloves to make her think I took a card. You would not do that with a three year old, at least not the first time you play! Also with a three year old use FAR fewer items - I suggest starting with only three items, preferably real objects as opposed to pictures.

If this had been with Anna (who likes to run the show) she would have asked for a turn. I didn't give Julie a turn because I wanted to show you different games, but in a real lesson I'd definitely ask her if she wanted a go at moving the items. This way you are really playing together rather than you just ordering them about the whole time.

5. Backwards Bullseye: (7:16) Sorry the light is not very good but I was limited as to where I could stick the pictures. The idea of this game is for Julie to repeatedly hear the phrase "I've forgotten my", and then have a turn at saying it. When Julie first says the phrase she says "I've forgot my bag". I immediately correct her because she's going to drill the phrase repeatedly and it must be done right, otherwise you are going to drill in an error. She keeps trying to say "I've forgot my..." for the first few goes. See the way I correct her, not by speaking but by indicating she's made a mistake and letting her correct herself. It's much more satisfying for her to correct herself and thus "get it right", rather than be corrected by me and have "gotten it wrong".

It goes without saying that if you don't want to get into this ridiculous position just use a variant such as aiming over your shoulder, or find some kind of movement that is acceptable to you and your culture.

6. Name and Chase: (8:56) I'm using this game for short dialogues. Before we play we rehearse the dialogue a couple of times and I make sure Julie is saying her part correctly. The "chase" card is the sunglasses in this game. Julie is much quicker the second time the sunglasses come up. In a real lesson I would have played this a few more times, and added in more "chase" cards to make the game more exciting. For example the sunglasses and the hat could be "chase" cards. Also I'd have let Julie take a turn turning the cards over.

7. Snap: (11:50) This game is another speaking game to run through the nouns and, because it uses word flashcards instead of pictures, it also introduces the spelling of these words to Julie. One always plays several games with word flashcards before expecting the pupil to be able to write the word, either in a writing game or on a work sheet. Julie realises what game we are going to play, it's called "Bataille" in French. She beats me fair and square at that without me pretending to be slow either!

8. Oranges: (13:55) A daft game really, the idea being to take the fruit, which is sitting on a flashcard on the table and carry it over to a matching flashcard somewhere else in the room. Really at this point in the lesson I was just doing a demo of the game for you - it was not necessary from a language point of view. After you've put all the fruits on the matching picture or word card the pupil can name all the words and count up how many they got on target. A benefit of this game is that it involves movement to break up the sitting in between Snap and Noughts and Crosses.

9. Noughts and Crosses or Tic Tac Toe: (14:35) We get ready by picking out five word cards each. Using word cards is another exposure to spelling. With younger children who are not learning reading and writing yet play the same game but with picture cards.

10. Putting an extended role-play together: (16:35) The language in the lesson has been leading up to putting on this role-play. This is called "Ready Steady Go" and it's available along with 26 other plays in an ebook that is available separately as a compliment to these games. The role-plays are for age 4 and upwards as they are too ambitious for the average three year old who is beginning in English. Note that before we get to this role-play we have learned ALL the language in it from memory and gone over it in listening and speaking games, and we've even seen how some of the words are spelled. This fact means that it's quite quick to put the role-play together - it only takes us about ten minutes. Afterwards we put it on to the mum, using a real car and the mum said "this is just what it's like every day when we leave for school!"

So the first run through I take Julie through the play as she does not know the plot/events. I feed her the lines. The two chairs are our bus/car, which I am driving and she's the passenger. At the end of the first run through I explain to her that I'm the driver and I've forgotten my keys. See how she understands me when I talk at normal speed with the aid of the context and the actions.

We run through it again and there's a short cut when we move the props to outside the room. I left it all in so you can see the whole process. When Julie goes off to get her gloves during the second run through she spends ages putting them on. This is CLASSIC, and the younger the kids the worse it gets. The children get so involved in the props that they really make the dialogue drag. So when I go and get my chauffeur's hat I tell her just to come in with the gloves as otherwise the play is boring for spectators and she quickly gets the point. With younger children I simplified the props, even removing them sometimes because otherwise things drag, which, I admit is more of a problem when you have a group of kids than in a one on one situation.

I've shown you all three run-throughs just so you have the full process. With younger children, or children who have not had a term of English at school already you'll probably go slower. In that case I recommend putting the play together over several sessions. Certainly Julie and I can further rehearse and refine our little skit in future lessons for fun, or put it on to family members. If you are a teacher do prepare things like this to show parents at the end of each term as the children love to show off and be the centre of attention while the parents are pleased to see some results and proof that some learning has been going on in the classes they are paying for. Plus it's great fun for all concerned!

JULIE GAMES DEMO VIDEO COMMENTARY

An hour long video showing different games in action. This is the first time Julie has played any of these games.

This lesson may be viewed online here:
http://www.homeenglishteacher.com/video/julie_games.html

Abracadanagram: (0:00) Play this with real objects, pictures or words. See how I correct Julie when she says "We likes" by repeating "We likes?" with a questioning tone so she knows it's wrong and she instantly corrects herself. When Julie says "It likes apple" she misses off the "s" on apples. I choose not to correct that but to repeat the phrase twice, clearly saying the "s" on apples so at least she's heard the correct version. I can't say that my way of doing things is the only way of course, it's my personal preference not to correct EVERYTHING because I've seen the effect that can have on a student's confidence.

Anagram Timebomb: (2:42) Unfortunately Julie loses both rounds of this so I didn't manage that very well. The first time Julie just answers questions and the second round she also has to ask them. This is a fluency game rather than a drill for accuracy so don't correct mistakes and help out if you need to to keep the ball rolling.

Anagrams: (5:09) Julie prepares some words for me to figure out, which gives her an opportunity to think about spelling. We are going to race each other unravelling our words. She wins all the time because I gave her words that we were working on in our lesson the day before, whereas she is giving me any word that she can think of. I use a paper clip to keep the letters together to save time. I beat Julie the first time as she has the b upside down and it looks like a q. Then she beats me hands down! Next time I play that with her I won't make it so easy for her.

Boggle: (8:36) When Julie hesitates I give her a clue, which is inaudible on the film, telling her there's a word there that is an item of clothing. We play till the bomb stops ticking. What I'd do in a normal lesson rather than a video demo is play three rounds of this, making a note of how many words we find each time as a team, and seeing if we do better each time. There's no point even trying to play this as a competition as you are always going to find more words than your pupil.

Anagram Waddle: (10:35) You can't see this very quick demonstration too clearly on the film but you'll figure it out if you read the game instructions as well. Julie beat me far too easily so in a real lesson I'd play again and not put myself at such a disadvantage, just to make it a bit closer as it's more fun then. This kind of thing you tweak depending on your child and how he or she reacts to games/winning/losing. Younger children hate losing but older ones can handle some losing, but they don't want to lose all the time, so you wangle it so that they win most of the time.

Bogeyman: (10:49) We've never played this before so we take a few goes to figure it out. I've left everything in so you see one way to handle things when a game does not go well. After trying for a few goes I simplify it where it's always the same person asking the question so we can get into a rhythm. That's often the solution if a game is not working: SIMPLIFY. Then I think up a variant with the hand slapping and that goes well right from the start.

Brainstorm: (14.36) Julie has to say one word to my two. See how I leave the obvious words to her, especially with the colours.

Clapping Game: (17:16) Also shown in Anna's lesson. Here's another example of how to use this game. This is another fluency game so it's not a time for corrections. We don't play for long as we are only doing a demo for you. It's hard this game, so in fact a good idea is to allow a whole clapping sequence between each speaker to give time to think of something, as otherwise it's very hard to keep up the rhythm - even I couldn't do it and I'm English!

Count The Cards: (18:14) The game goes well, especially considering it's the first time we played it. Julie has some useful counting revision at the end totalling her points.

Blind Directions: (20:20) Julie's a bit old for this game but it's still useful for listening to directions/commands. Younger children will get more of a kick out of it.

Duck Duck Goose: (22:15 This was an experiment as I've never played Duck Duck Goose with only one person before. It will work really well with a younger child. With some tweaks I think this would work better by getting rid of the chairs, which slowed us down too much. Big cushions on the floor or racing to throw ourselves on the sofa when we get to "fox". Have fun experimenting with the idea!

Find The Pairs Memory Game: (23:06) We use this game for descriptive words and the order of them "big, brown lions", but use it for any language or with word cards. (It's better with pictures.) Try mixing up pictures and word cards together. This is more of a language drill type of game so it's good to correct things here.

Fizz Buzz: (28:00) After the first round I prepare to make it harder but Julie says no, so I thrown in the "time bomb" device to add some spice. We would have played again in a real lesson. If a game is fun play it for longer, but don't wear it out, that way it will still be fun at future sessions.

Flip A Card: (28:59) The piece of paper we are consulting during this game tells us which letter corresponds to the playing card. So and card with 1 corresponds to the letters C and D (on our chart), 2 is E and F and so on - see the game description for full details. When I turn over cards I try not to say the most obvious word, so for example when I turn over a 9, which corresponds with S and T, I don't say "two" or "table" - easy words I leave for Julie, but say "Titanic". If I'd been with a four year old child I would not have said "Titanic" as a four year old would not know that film/historic event. So say things that are relevant to your pupil as much as possible.

I use this game to mention some new words to Julie, which she can understand from my mime or because they are close to the French. English and French both stem from Indo-European so many words are quite similar. You won't have this advantage if you are teaching a totally unrelated language so in that case you might not want to be so adventurous with your choice of words but pick ones your pupil is already familiar with, or use lots of mime to make any meanings clear.

Guess The Word: (32:32) I start to spell a word and Julie has to guess what it is. She gets 100 points if she guesses on the first letter, 50 on the second and so on. Notice how I give her words I know she knows like those we covered in the Ready Steady Go lesson or the lesson today. I noted that Julie could use some work on the alphabet so I'd do that in a future lesson.

Hangman: (35:31) Julie gets the first word so easily that I change the rules and say you have to get three words before the hangman is complete. I give her easy words I'm sure she knows, and two words we've covered today: rabbit and gloves. As she got the first two so easily I changed the rules again and did not give her a clue for the third letter. This game, like Guess the Word just above, is giving Julie some well-needed work on the alphabet.

Hidden Picture: (46:04)

Prepositions: (48:56) You don't need those exact same sticks with coloured stripes to play this. See the game description for an idea using playing cards instead, still practising prepositions. I pull the sticks out as it slows you down and gives Julie the edge. During the game Julie has an idea for a variant. Always be ready to try out your pupil's game ideas as it's a great way to learn new ones that way and also to find out what your pupil finds fun.

Higher Or Lower: (56:16)

OTHER RESOURCES

I hope that these plays are great fun for you and your pupils. Here are my other resources, which may be useful if you teach a variety of ages or class sizes. Do check my website or email me to find out if any new ones have come out since purchasing this book.

1. English Language Games for Children: ESL Games for the primary age.

The perfect companion to these plays, plenty of games to pre-teach vocabulary and grammar in the skits using games.

Available on various Amazon websites as a physical book. Search for:
ESL Games: English Language Games for Children Shelley Ann Vernon
Currently on Amazon.com, Amazon.co.uk, Amazon.es, Amazon.fr, Amazon.de

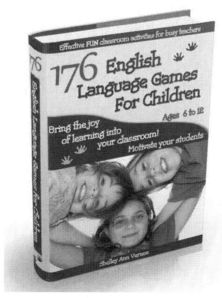

2. Vocabulary flashcards in popular themes

Currently PDF downloads from www.teachingenglishgames.com

They may become available as physical flashcards in future.

3. Preschool Games and Stories 1 to 10

Ten stories covering basic vocabulary themes and useful vocabulary with a fun games book for preschoolers.

www.teachingenglishgames.com/3-5.htm

4. English for Nursery: How to Teach English as a Second Language to two year old children.

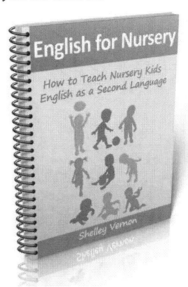

5. Teaching English Songs 1 2 and 3 - CDs or Download

This CD contains sixteen songs to match the vocabulary taught in my preschool stories series. The words are simple, covering basic vocabulary themes, helping you to reinforce what you are teaching while bringing cheerful   music   to   the   classroom.

A songs activity book is included with CD 1, lesson plan ideas for introducing and teaching each song. The ideas in there may be used with any songs in the series. In addition masks of all the characters in the story are included in black and white, to cut out, colour and wear, and pre-coloured. The fox shown is not to scale. These could be used for the Zoo Talk play.

www.teachingenglishgames.com/eslsongs.htm
&
www.teachingenglishgames.com/eslsongs3.htm

6. 10 x Follow-on Stories 11 to 20 with Lesson Plans

More stories covering actions, family members, rooms of the house, nature, light and dark, verbs, farm animals, body parts, clothing and other useful vocabulary.

www.teachingenglishgames.com/3-5/preschoolstories.htm

7. 10 x Stories for Special Days in the Year

Stories with lesson plans, flashcards, colouring and illustrations

Birthday	Ground hog Day	April Fools' Day
Halloween	Valentine's Day	Mother's Day
Thanksgiving	Easter Bunny	Summer Holiday Adventure
Christmas		

Includes revision of vocabulary and grammar from stories one to twenty, plus new words, language and tenses.

www.teachingenglishgames.com/eslstory.htm

8. Fun Role-Plays and Skits for Children Learning English

30 easy fun skits available from my website in PDF and on Amazon.

For videos of plays in action please see this post on my blog:

http://teachingenglishgames.blogspot.fr/2012/03/watch-these-fun-esl-skits-for-kids.html

And these notes from a Dragica in Macedonia who is using the plays, to see how she got on with them and her comments.

http://teachingenglishgames.blogspot.fr/2012/03/esl-role-plays-and-skits-get-inspired.html

9. Teen Adult language games

ABOUT THE AUTHOR

Following her BA degree in languages at Durham University, England in 1989 Shelley Vernon took a TEFL qualification and became a teacher. She taught in language schools in the UK and privately around the world for several years.

Having been largely bored to death herself while in school Shelley was determined not to put her own students through the same desperate clock-watching and she always strove to prepare fun, stimulating classes that pupils would enjoy and remember. She taught using a variety of methods, including the driest textbooks imaginable, which called for large amounts of creativity in order to make lessons more interesting. However it was only when she started to teach children in 1999 that she really discovered how much fun teaching can be.

She created resources from her experiences and has shared her ideas with thousands of teachers around the world, bringing enthusiasm and a love of learning, as well as great results into the classroom. Shelley's approach concentrates on enhancing listening and speaking skills through language games which involve repetition and through fluency activities which have genuine communicative value rather than artificial conversation.

She created her best-selling "English Language Games for Children" and followed this up with resources for preschool children, including games and a curriculum laid out in thirty illustrated stories. Having taught preschool children at a Montessori nursery Shelley knows exactly what a teacher needs to do this successfully and stories are a stunningly useful element. Her ESL Games and Activities for Adults are also highly praised by teachers around the world.

In addition to her degree in foreign languages, Shelley also holds a university degree in music (2000) from Canterbury Christchurch College. She lives in France, because of the nice weather, loves classical music, and enjoys keeping fit with skiing, yoga, singing and walking her adorable cocker spaniel. She also writes songs and has 3 preschool songs CDs. She speaks occasionally at conferences. (IATEFL Cardiff 2009 and YALS Belgrade 2011)

Made in the USA
Lexington, KY
28 January 2018